D1558579

Cloud
CHALLENGE
of the
STALLIONS

FRONT RANGE EQUINE RESCUE

Happy Trails!

Ginger Kathrens

SAVING AMERICA'S MUSTANGS

Cloud

CHALLENGE of the STALLIONS

The saga of the wild horses of the Arrowheads continues in this companion book to public television's NATURE program.

by *Ginger Kathrens*

For Raven, who invited me into his mysterious and beautiful world and taught me the value of freedom and family. There will never be another like you.

For Sitka, lead mare extraordinaire who took care of Cloud for as long as she could.

For Dusty, who inspires me every day to prevent the senseless death of any wild horse.

And for all those wild spirits who roam in my memory and my heart.

Additional photographs reproduced with permission: © Living Images by Carol Walker, pp. cover, iv, 36, 44, 55, 58, 63, 72, 100, 105, 117, 145, 146, 149, 150, 152, 153; Thomas Homburg, p 15; Ann Evans, pp. 15,21, 27, 35-36-37 (BG), 60, 67, 70, 90, 93, 136-140 (BG); © Deb Little, pp. ii, 16, 20, 24, 55, 58, 59, 64, 74, 75, 77, 78, 79, 80, 81, 85, 95, 96, 98, 102, 111, 113, 129, 130, 131; © Pam Nickoles, pp. 106, 129, 134, 137, 141; © Makendra Silverman/The Cloud Foundation, pp. 23, 68, 73, 80, 83-85, 90, 92, 99, 100, 110, 112-114, 116, 118, 120, 122-125, 139, 140, 143-145; Nancy Cerroni/The Pryor Mountain Wild Mustang Center, p. 29; Tony Wengert, pp. 148, Back Cover "Racing the Wind"; MillersReflections Photography, Back Cover-Ginger, Trace, and Connor.

The Cloud Foundation, Inc.
A Colorado 501(c)3
107 South 7th Street
Colorado Springs, Colorado 80905

Printed and bound in Canada by Friesens Corporation
2nd Edition

ISBN-13: 978-0-615-37652-3

A Word of Thanks
The book, Cloud: Challenge of the Stallions, was made possible through the generous help of Front Range Equine Rescue and Marian Jo Souder. Many of the photographs in this book were donated to The Cloud Foundation by these talented individuals who care about preserving wild horses in the wild: Ann Evans, Thomas Homberg, Deb Little, Jody Miller, Pam Nickoles, Makendra Silverman, Carol Walker and Tony Wengert.

I would like to thank WNET in New York City for funding the Nature series on PBS; and for helping to bring Cloud's life story to viewers around the world.

Author's Note:
While a number of my journeys into Cloud's home were solo adventures, many trips were made with friends and colleagues who have greatly contributed to the making of the Cloud books and films. You know who you are and I hope you know how much I value your dedication, hard work, companionship, counsel, support and love. Happy Trails to you always!

Editor: Anni Williams

Additional Editorial Consultants: Makendra Silverman, Ann Evans, Christine Ferguson

Designer: Kyla Umemoto Grantham

Contents

Introduction

When Raven and his family brought a tottering newborn out of the trees in front of my camera on May 29, 1995, it was an unforgettable moment. The colt was nearly white, and I named him Cloud. At first sight, I felt an instant affection for him and sensed his charismatic personality. My first two books and the Nature series on PBS chronicle much of Cloud's life. But many of the events I describe in this new tale were set in motion the year before Cloud was born.

In March of 1994, my sister, Marian, and I got up before dawn to try to find a wild horse band in the Arrowhead Mountains on the Montana/Wyoming border. We were on a location scouting trip for a Wild America film about mustangs, and we had heard about the birth of a new foal in a band led by a black stallion named Raven. Despite our total lack of experience with wild horses and our complete lack of knowledge about the area, we set out to find the foal. The horse range was only 40,000 acres. *How hard could it be?*

As the sun rose over the Bighorn Mountains, we saw a black stallion eating snow at the base of a red butte. Nearby, a pale gray, newborn foal walked in the sage with his buckskin mother, two other mares and a yearling. I knew we had found Raven and his family. Although they all ran away from us, I felt an unusual connection to the black stallion. At the time, I had no idea that my

The BLM freeze branded Shaman in preparation for his sale to a Cody, Wyoming outfitter.

encounter with him would change my life forever.

In the months that followed, Raven and his beautiful trio of mares opened their world to me. For some strange reason, they allowed me to travel their well-worn horse trails with them and to discover what being a wild horse is all about. I learned that they value their families and their freedom above all else. By June, two more foals had been born to the family, and I fell in love with all three of Raven's lively little sons. Like a sponge, I soaked up as much knowledge and understanding of the horses as I could in this one, brief, magical summer.

I also learned how the Bureau of Land Management manages wild horses on our public lands. As a result of a BLM roundup that fall, two of Raven's foals died along with wild horses from other family bands. It was hard for me to believe that creatures so beautiful could be treated so cruelly.

The BLM also captured many of the band stallions. They planned to sell them so that younger stallions could participate in the breeding. This, too, boggled my mind. Although I'm not a trained scientist, I have a lifelong love and understanding of animals, and I'm keenly interested in the natural history of all wildlife species. I understand the skill, courage, intelligence, and physical prowess it takes to become a successful breeder in the wild. Removing the very stallions that had proven their ability to pass on these qualities to the next generation was a terrible idea. Had the BLM never heard of *survival of the fittest* or *natural selection?*

With the help of Karen Sussman, President of the International Society for the Protection of Mustangs and Burros, and Trish Kerby, a wild horse lover and area resident, we were able to convince the BLM of this error in judgment. They released all the band stallions—all but one that is. The BLM had promised the dun band stallion Shaman to a Cody, Wyoming outfitter who planned to use this proud and dominant stallion as a pack animal. Karen called me to ask if I thought Shaman should go to the outfitter in order for the BLM to save face. "It's your decision," she said. I replied, "Tell them to set him free." They released him the next morning.

If Shaman had gone to the outfitter rather than back into the wild, the remarkable story that follows would never have happened.

Author's Note: *Cloud: Challenge of the Stallions* covers five years (June 2003 to August of 2008) in the life of Cloud and the wild horses of the Arrowheads.

Chapter 1

Winning Velvet

The distant, unmistakable screams of wild stallions pierced the fog atop the Arrowhead Mountains ... and I followed their haunting calls. Another shriek echoed through the misty pine forest, and I hiked faster. At the edge of ancient limestone cliffs, I looked down through a fast moving veil of clouds into a teacup-shaped meadow. Two horses emerged from the fog.

The wild stallions slid to a stop and faced off against each other, standing upright on their hind legs. Like boxers in a super heavyweight bout, they struck at each other with their front hooves. I recognized both stallions immediately. One was a slender bay bachelor who had broken his pastern (the horse version of our ankle) years ago but learned to run again with barely a limp. The other was a compact red roan band stallion I have known since he was a foal. It was Cloud's brother, Red Raven, fighting to hold onto his two blue roan mares, Blue Sioux and Adona.

Red Raven lashed out with his front hooves, then swiveled, screamed in anger, and delivered a kick to the ribs of the taller but slower bay. Red Raven's mares continued grazing, hardly paying any attention, confident that Red Raven had everything under control. The older bay was testing Red Raven and he got his answer. If he wanted to win a mare, it would not be from Red

Raven who would fight to the death to hold onto his small family. The bachelor reluctantly backed away.

Red Raven's family is one of over 30 wild horse families in the Arrowhead Mountains of southern Montana. Each family is also called a band. The male leader of the family is the band stallion, and he has one or more mares as well as their young offspring.

It was early June and the snows had receded on the lower ridges. Many of the bands had traveled uphill, following the greening grass. The first good high elevation grazing is the lovely round teacup bowl surrounded by dramatic snow-rimmed cliffs. Typical of this time of year, mares were foaling and coming into heat, setting off a frenzy of stallion activity. Band stallions were on high alert. At any time, a bachelor or band stallion trying to steal their mares might challenge them.

The fog gradually lifted, and I was excited to discover other horses in the bowl. Near a huge snowdrift below the cliffs, I spotted Cloud's palomino son, Bolder. He had turned two years old just days before. Bolder sported the last of his dead, whitish winter coat, but I could see his golden color emerging. And he was still with his stepfather Shaman, the mares, and a newborn foal.

Shaman grazed near the mare and their baby. I had admired the mighty dun stallion for nearly a decade. He was fierce in battle, but nurturing with his mares. Three years before, Cloud had stolen a black mare from the injured band stallion Plenty Coups. As an immature five-year-old, he was not yet strong enough or savvy enough to hang onto her when challenged by a dominant male like Shaman who stole the mare. But before Shaman stole her, Cloud bred the mare ... and the golden colt in the valley below was the result of that brief encounter. And so, Bolder was born into Shaman's band and knew no other father than this powerful yet gentle stallion.

As I watched, I noticed Bolder sniffing Shaman's mare who was with the new foal. The palomino lifted his upper lip and inhaled, a behavior known as flehmen. The mare was in heat and Bolder

Bolder lifted his lip in a behavior known as flehmen.

could smell her intoxicating aroma. *Surely, Shaman had seen him too,* I thought. I anticipated that he would discipline Bolder. Instead, he turned his head away and yawned. "Strange," I whispered. When Cloud was not yet two, his father Raven had kicked him out of the family to eliminate any competition for breeding rights. I knew of two sons Shaman had kicked out as two-year-olds. *What was so special about Bolder?* I wondered why he allowed him to stay, and why Bolder wanted to. At this time in his life, he should be with other bachelor stallions, practicing the fighting skills required to one day win a mare.

The sun rose higher over the snow-covered Bighorn Mountains to the east, burning off the last of the fog in the bowl. The sunlight glinted in Shaman's amber eyes as he looked up. We both heard distant shrieks. Just over the big hill, beyond the bowl, stallions were fighting and the battle sounded serious. I started hiking, excited to find out what was going on.

When I crested the hill, I saw Cloud and his band. The pale palomino I had followed since his birth eight years earlier now grazed beside his blue roan lead mare, Sitka, and her two-year-old son Flint. Sitka had been Shaman's lead mare in 1994 when I first ventured into their world. In 2000, Cloud somehow stole her from Shaman. I can't imagine how he pulled this off, but he did. When he won her, the mare was already pregnant. And the following July, Flint was born into Cloud's little family.

What a strange and surprising turnabout! Cloud and Shaman ended up raising each other's sons. And how ironic it was that both two-year-old stepsons were still being tolerated in their stepfathers' bands.

As I moved closer, I saw Cloud staring intently at bachelors circling a family band. Sitka, too, looked up from grazing as if realizing that something ominous was about to happen. Not just one bachelor stallion but six young males pursued the stylish dun stallion, Prince, and his band of three mares, a pair of two-year-old fillies, and a new foal. The aggressive bachelors circled

13

Prince looked thin and tired.

the family like a pack of wolves, testing and assessing the weakness of the stallion. I had never seen this kind of behavior before with so many bachelors appearing to work together to shatter one family band.

Prince dipped his head low to the ground in a behavior called snaking and drove the mares away from the bachelors. Then, whenever Prince turned to fight off one of the bachelors, the others moved in, driving his mares away. Prince would react by racing back to intercept the team of bachelors and recover his mares. I didn't know how long this contest had been going on, but judging by Prince's bedraggled appearance, it must have started days before. The lightly built stallion looked thin and tired; yet, he was gallantly hanging onto his family.

Standing with his band in the midst of the melee, Cloud went back to grazing. That the bachelors did not attempt to steal any members of his family told me Cloud had matured enough to discourage potential challengers.

Then, without any warning, Cloud's head shot up and he galloped off. He had noticed that Prince's dun mare had moved a few steps from her band, and he charged full speed toward her.

Prince gallantly hangs on to his family as Cloud watches.

Just as he moved in to drive her away, Prince dove at him, biting at his rump. Cloud whirled, kicked at Prince, and then shot out after the rest of Prince's band. But before he could cut out a mare, a black bachelor jumped him. As Cloud fought off the black, he realized that two other bachelors were making off with his unattended family and he raced back, driving the would-be thieves away. My head was spinning as I tried to keep up with the pace and complexity of the action.

Cloud and his band settled once more into grazing when I spotted a dun bachelor driving the two-year-old black filly in Prince's family in the direction of Cloud's band. Cloud watched the dun and the filly closely. When they raced by, he attacked the terrified bachelor who pivoted, running for his life with Cloud on his heels. With the dun in full retreat, Cloud hurried back to the filly, easing her into his family. The nervous filly whinnied for her mother. I knew the filly's mother well. She was the blue roan mare in Prince's band.

Eight years before, a black filly had come to visit Raven and his trio of foals, which included two-week-old Cloud. As the only foal in her small band, the filly may have been lonely and wanted a

playmate. She ventured to within a few yards of the band. When little Cloud saw her, he lowered his head and laid his ears flat against his head, imitating the snaking behavior of adult stallions he had been watching so carefully. But instead of leading her closer to him as he expected, he ended up scaring her away. At first, I named the filly Black Velvet. In time, she roaned out ... her black body hair mixing with white, giving the coat a bluish appearance. As she developed into a blue roan color, I began calling her just Velvet.

Cloud whirled and kicked out at Prince.

Cloud positioned himself between Velvet and the rest of the band.

Now, I was watching the grown-up Cloud as he focused his attentions on the lovely adult mare Velvet. He had captured her black daughter, and I believed he knew he had a chance to win Velvet, too. After all, she would want to be with her daughter and vice-versa. This might give him the edge he needed.

In a bold move, Cloud left his band and raced toward Prince, surprising him with the speed of his attack. They scuffled briefly before Cloud darted away, positioning himself between Velvet and the rest of the band. He bit at her rear and she burst into a gallop, squirting liquid as she ran. Velvet was in heat.

While Cloud was off chasing Velvet, three bachelors attacked Sitka and the band. Flint tried to defend his mother, standing his ground in front of the tall, red roan who was over twice his age and seemed twice his size. Despite Flint's good intentions, he was no match for the stallion. When the red roan charged at him, Flint spun around, running away as fast as he could … with the roan and a vicious looking black bachelor biting at his rump. He raced to his mother, Sitka, who was leading the band away as the bachelors chased after them. She led the family in a circle back toward Cloud and Velvet. When the band was close, Cloud raced out and knocked off one of the bachelors. But when he left, Velvet dashed off, rejoining Prince. Cloud had a split second decision to make – whether to rescue his family from the bachelors or pursue Velvet. He chose Velvet.

Cloud galloped toward Velvet, chasing off two bachelors along the way. Then he cut Velvet

The bachelors reared and viciously bit at each other.

out of Prince's band again. Racing side by side, Cloud and Velvet joined up with her daughter, and the three stopped running. Mother and daughter stood huddled together as Cloud paced nervously around them.

Sitka and the band disappeared over a far hill. *Oh no,* I thought, *you've made a big mistake.* Had Cloud lost his family in order to win Velvet?

Then Sitka, Flint, and the rest of the band suddenly reappeared over the hill. Sitka kicked at the three bachelors who were trying to drive them away from the main field of battle. Interestingly, she made a looping right turn. The canny old mare was more in control than it looked.

With the bachelors in hot pursuit, she whinnied. Cloud answered her call but stayed close to Velvet and her daughter. I think Sitka heard his reply and adjusted her direction immediately. Galloping and kicking at the three bachelors, she whinnied again. Cloud responded as if to say, "I'm down here!"

Sitka barreled downhill toward Cloud and, when his family was within a hundred feet of him, he reacted, galloping full speed toward the bachelors who mounted only a token defense before they scattered like leaves in a windstorm. Perhaps out of sheer frustration, one of the black bachelors started a fight with the red roan stallion. They viciously bit at each other and spun in circles, then reared and kicked. This was an unwise move on their part, for it gave Cloud some quiet time to introduce both Velvet and her daughter to their new family.

Once Cloud's band was all together, the bachelors stopped challenging him. Instead, they turned their attentions back to Prince. Over time, the gallant stallion wore out, and his remaining mares ended up with two separate bachelor stallions, the young dun and one of the blacks. And, Cloud finally captured Velvet, the foal he tried to win eight years before.

When Cloud chose to pursue Velvet, leaving his family with the bachelors, I believe he knew that his steady, lead mare Sitka, would find a way to bring his family back to him. If Sitka had rejected Velvet and her daughter by kicking at them, as I had seen mares do when their stallion brought a new mare home, it is unlikely that Cloud could have kept them together. But not once did I see Sitka act as if Velvet and her daughter were unwelcome. Clearly, Sitka was a remarkable leader and an invaluable mate to Cloud.

Late in the day, I watched Cloud courting Velvet as warm light bathed the distant snow-covered Bighorn Mountains.

Chapter 2

Dancing in the Arrowheads

I watched Dancer race at sunset.

A few weeks later, I returned hoping to see if Cloud's expanded family was still together. I reached the mountaintop at sunset. Deep purple lupine speckled the open green meadows. As I drove on the road and crested the high hill that dropped toward an old cabin, I stopped. There were horses near the road. I got out to take a closer look with my binoculars. I could see a group of unidentifiable dark horses. When a pale horse walked in to join the others, the group became instantly recognizable. It was Cloud and his band! Then I noticed something tiny racing around the trees – a little foal. Quickly, I jumped back into the car and drove closer.

Despite all the running and kicking the month before, Sitka had delivered a filly foal who appeared perfect ... although much smaller than the average Arrowhead newborn. The dark baby with a white star and snip was about the size of a big dog. I watched her race at sunset, galloping at top speed in and around the clusters of firs. She stopped and stared at me ... and I waved a friendly hello, my signal to her that I wasn't trying to sneak up on her and meant her no harm. In response, she jumped into the air, did a pirouette, and danced on as the light faded. I named her Cloud Dancer ... just Dancer for short.

The next day, Cloud and the band moved away from the tiny mountaintop cabin named for Penn Cummings, the young cowboy who built it in the

1920s. The band dropped into a valley where the old stallion Bigfoot lived in the summer. I found them in a secluded meadow full of lupine flowers. In the trees, a mature mule deer buck eyed me suspiciously. But after hours of sitting with Cloud and his family, the buck let his guard down and foraged near me. Soft velvet covered his impressive rack of multi-tined antlers. The velvet was full of blood vessels that helped keep him cool in summer. In the fall, the velvet would be shed and his antlers would become a weapon to help him win does.

Cloud looked up at the buck, then went back to grazing. Dancer sauntered toward her father while opening and closing her mouth and clacking her teeth together. Her submissive gesture translated into, "Please don't hurt me. I'm not just little, I'm really tiny." Then she precociously raced away, winding her way around the firs and back into a clearing, darting this way and that. She might be small, but she had attitude. Dancer was definitely the product of an exceptionally strong mother and father. There would be no pushing this spirited little girl around. However, spirit and attitude would not be enough to prevent predation. Even the strongest foals would die that summer. Mountain lion predation, which began in earnest in 2001 when Flint and Bolder were born, was on the rise. I feared that tiny Dancer would be among the missing.

Shaman and Cloud did not drive their two-year-old sons from their families. Were they making conscious decisions to keep these young stallions at home?

Other less menacing questions plagued me during the summer as well. Shaman and Cloud had not driven their two-year-old stepsons away from their bands. *Why not? Were they making conscious decisions to keep these young stallions at home – perhaps to help detect a hunting cougar?*

Bolder wandered off many times to play with bachelors, most of them older than he. After a while, either he would race back to his family, or Shaman would go out and snake him home with

Flint stayed home more, choosing to play fight with Bolder.

Bolder mouthing in submission like a tiny foal. Flint, on the other hand, stayed home more and played infrequently with the bachelors, choosing instead to play fight with Bolder. And he had plenty of opportunities!

That summer the two bands began to stay closer together. *Was this a response to intensifying predation?* The herd's behavior reminded me of the time I filmed Common Zebras in Kenya. They live in family groups like our American wild horses. With zebras, however, it is hard to tell one family group from another since the bands hang out in large herds, affording them safety in numbers. Perhaps African zebras and the wild horses of Montana had something in common. *Were Shaman and Cloud's families sensing that this was a valuable survival strategy?*

In the fall when I returned to the mountain, I found Cloud and his family with little Dancer. Once again, they had traveled their well-beaten trails from the designated horse range to the higher elevations in the national forest. This was not a new pattern for the wild horses of the Arrowheads; for hundreds of years, they have journeyed to the highest meadows where snow lingers the longest and grass under the trees is still green.

When I hiked closer, I could see Cloud grooming with a new mare, a lovely grulla filly with a tiny star on her head. She was the three-year-old daughter of Black Beauty and Beauty, a Spanish

21

looking stallion and mare who lived much of the year far below … in the desert country next to the Bighorn Canyon. As Cloud and the young mare groomed affectionately, I wondered if Cloud won the filly or if she chose him. Flint looked up from grazing, surveying them. I could tell he thought the filly was pretty, too. Her name was Aztec, and like all grullas, she was a gray color with a dorsal stripe and stripes on the back of her front legs.

Gradually, the band moved in the direction of the spring-fed water hole. They leisurely drank, splashed a bit, and then walked north toward the huge escarpment overlooking the Crow Indian Reservation. Cloud's home was once the sacred heart of Crow Indian country. On the edge of the escarpment, vision quest sites (stacks of rocks piled in a horseshoe-shape) still grace the cliff edges. Young Native American boys once stood in them and stared out at the hills far below. They would fast, waiting for a vision or for an animal to appear which would be their totem throughout life – a

Gradually, the band moved in the direction of the spring-fed water hole.

22

sacred animal that would protect and guide them.

I stood near one vision quest site and stared out at the rock outcroppings below, and then I surveyed the canopy of trees, broken by open, electric green meadows. Small, abandoned ponds dotted the forest meadows, created by beavers who once lived there. The endless, rolling hills of the Crow Indian Reservation lay beyond.

In the boulder field just below me, something dashed in and out of the rocks. It was a long-tailed weasel bouncing athletically from one rock to another ... hunting for mice and anything else it could kill and consume. The 10-ounce predator is one of the most fearsome of all hunters, taking prey far larger than itself. *Was the pint-sized predator my totem animal? And, if so, how might I interpret this sign?* I smiled, imagining that this sleek cinnamon weasel might be my protector. It sat up for a few seconds and I could see its tiny dark eyes and pointed nose. He glanced around and then darted away.

On the edge of the escarpment, vision quest sites still grace the cliff edges.

I looked up when I heard the whir of wind through tapered wings. A white-throated swift, a swallow-like bird considered the fighter jet of the avian world, zoomed by. With incredible velocity, it was seizing tiny insects in mid-air, diving and banking, then rising again into the deep blue sky.

As the afternoon light deepened, I walked away from the escarpment and found Bolder nearby playing with a black bachelor much older than himself. Shaman and the band were far off on the other side of the water hole, and I wondered if Bolder had finally joined the ranks of the raucous bachelor boys. He was certainly holding his own with the spirited black. They ran and bucked, then stopped, bending low and nipping at each other's front legs. I watched them for hours believing that Bolder was finally out on his own. Then his head shot up, and he began running. In a matter of seconds, Bolder had crossed the wide meadows, galloping back to his family. *What an athlete* I thought. I had never seen a wild horse run that fast.

In the minutes just before sunset, I found Cloud and Flint standing side by side with Aztec. They watched many bands walking from the water hole toward the escarpment. Red Raven and his mares, Adona and Blue Sioux, walked by with their colt, a pretty blaze-faced chestnut. The colt approached little Dancer hesitantly. Cloud's daughter had roaned out. White hairs now outnumbered black ones, creating a silvery blue roan color. The tiny filly laid her ears back menacingly at the colt when they briefly touched noses. He got the message and backed away from her before she could kick him. Then he raced off to play with a sorrel colt. The two young males bucked and dashed around the trees as the sun dipped behind the horizon.

The next morning, I returned to the spring-fed water hole and heard whinnies. Seconds later, Blue Sioux, Red Raven, and Adona

*The beautiful chestnut colt
had simply disappeared.*

crested the hill above me. Blue Sioux whinnied as she trotted downhill. She stopped and whinnied again. She was searching for her son. I started looking for him too, walking in wider and wider circles from the place where I had last seen him. By the end of the day, Blue Sioux stopped searching and so did I. The beautiful chestnut colt had simply disappeared. I found nothing ... not a bone, a spot of blood or a piece of hair. This was not the first time that I had experienced a foal disappearing overnight. I felt sorry for Blue Sioux. She is such a good mother and so devoted to Red Raven.

Hard as it was to see the foals one day and not the next, I realize that it is nature's plan, developed over millions of years to balance predator and prey. Still, it was sad. That year, mountain lions killed most of the foals on the mountain. Feisty little Dancer was one of seven lucky survivors.

By fall Dancer's coat had roaned out.

25

Most of the horses grazed on the lower, windswept ridges.

Chapter 3

Sole Survivor

I spotted Bolder sparring with the bachelor stallion Shane.

2004 was a year unlike any other I had experienced in a decade of tracking wild horses in the Arrowheads. That spring I traveled up Tillett Ridge, one of two giant ridges separated by a deep canyon called Big Coulee. The two big ridges splintered into many smaller ridges, like the fingers of a gnarled hand. Because deep snow covered the high country, most of the horses grazed on these lower, wind swept ridges.

I spotted Bolder on Tillett playing with the bachelor stallion Shane. He had turned nearly white again, but his dead winter coat looked ready to fall out. *Was Bolder on his own?* I wondered. Since Tillett Ridge was not Shaman's territory, I felt increasingly confident that he had finally kicked the three-year-old out. Bolder joined other bachelors, I reasoned, and they wandered from Sykes Ridge to the smaller, sister ridge of Tillett. How wrong I was. As Bolder sparred with Shane, nipping at his face and legs, I saw Shaman coming. *Time to come home now,* Shaman

Bolder and Texas were a beautiful young couple, but I could not conceive of a scenario in which he could win the filly.

signaled, snaking with his head held only inches from the ground. Bolder promptly and obediently left the dun bachelor and returned to his mother and the band.

Many bachelor stallions roamed the mountain. Perhaps Shaman and Cloud were keeping their stepsons around not just to detect cats, but also to deflect the attack of marauding bachelors. Flint did act a bit like a lieutenant stallion, going out with Cloud, not only to play with the bachelors but also to warn them to stay away.

Late in the summer, Shaman won a new filly – a pretty four-year-old dun with a star and black and white domino-type markings just above her hooves. Bolder was clearly smitten. He would graze near the filly, walk with the filly, accompany the filly to water, and sometimes just stare at the filly. I called her Texas for the star on her forehead, shaped just like the state of Texas.

When winter came, Shaman's band stayed on Tillett Ridge rather than Sykes. *Why had they shifted ridges? Was Tillett safer? Perhaps the mountain lions were hunting on Sykes.* I watched Bolder graze in the snow with Texas. They were a beautiful young couple, but I could not conceive of a scenario in which Bolder could win the filly from his dominant stepfather.

Shaman had three foals that year and Cloud and Velvet had a pale buckskin filly, the color of Cloud's grandmother. They were four of twenty-nine born. All of the foals on the mountain top died that summer, fall, and winter. I was sure that most were killed by cougars.

Only one foal survived. He was a bright bay with a tomahawk marking on his head. The colt had been born and raised near the main gate into the horse range along a paved highway. It was a well-traveled road, and I think the secretive mountain lions avoided the area since they could be spotted there so easily. It was strange and sad to see band after band on the ridges and mountaintop with no babies. In time, however, I knew the horses would adapt their behavior to the intense predation. Their survival instincts, honed over millions of years of evolution, would kick in, and a natural balance of predator and prey would prevail.

Only one bay colt survived.

All of the foals on the mountain top died that summer, fall, and winter.

Deep snow still blanketed the mountaintop.

Chapter 4

Renewal

In May, I traveled up Tillett Ridge in search of horses. As deep snow still blanketed the mountaintop, I knew that the horses would be down on the lower ridges. I hoped that 2005 would be a year in which new foals would replace the tremendous losses of the year before. Above an area I call the mines (a distinctive red hill that had been an unsuccessful uranium mining area in the 1950s), I hiked downhill toward the edge of Big Coulee and sat on a rock ledge. I began glassing with my binoculars, looking for Cloud and his family on Sykes Ridge.

It was early afternoon and the sun was over my shoulder, perfect light to see horses on the distant hilltops. I began dissecting the ridges, one at a time, from the top to the bottom where they tumbled abruptly into the canyon. Almost immediately, a white object shone like a beacon atop the ridge. *Cloud!* Seeing the pale stallion is always a thrill. I set my spotting scope up on a small tripod and focused in closer.

The rest of the band came into sight, and I began counting noses; two-year old Dancer and four-year old Flint were still with the family as were their mother, Sitka, five-year-old Aztec, Velvet, and Velvet's big, four-year-old black daughter, a filly I called The Black. Near Velvet's feet, I could make out something orange, maybe just a dead juniper bush. Their branches often

turned a burnt orange when they died. I zoomed in on the small spot and refocused. The juniper got up and walked to Velvet. It was an orange foal!

Excitedly, I tried to memorize the landmarks around the horses ... the rock outcropping, a line of trees, a hilltop with a fallen old tree looking like a tangled skeleton ... so I could locate the band again when I drove up on Sykes. Thoughts raced through my brain. It would take me three or four hours to get down Tillett and up Sykes, and Cloud's family might be gone by then. And I would need to go into Lovell, Wyoming, to get gas. It would be foolhardy to start up treacherous Sykes Ridge without a full tank. With the trip into town, I still calculated that I could be there by nightfall. I would sleep in my SUV and have the next day to try to find them. Or, I could keep on exploring Tillett and go up on Sykes the next day.

As I mulled over my options, I continued to look through my scope and made yet another discovery. Something dark was moving around the mares; it was a newborn foal, hardly able to walk! *Was it the grulla filly's baby?* I wondered. But I could hardly believe my eyes when the dark foal tottered to Sitka and started to nurse. The Bureau of Land Management (BLM), the government agency in charge of managing wild horses on public lands, wanted to keep the population in Cloud's herd low and had been darting mares with the experimental infertility drug PZP, including 16-year-old Sitka. In spite of the drug, Sitka had given birth. The misguided infertility darting would prove to be one in a series of mistakes made by the BLM in their persistent attempts to manipulate nature.

*The scolding rattle of a
pine squirrel startled me.*

Any doubts about what to do next disappeared. By late afternoon,
I was back creeping up treacherous Sykes Ridge Road and hoping
the band was near the landmarks I had so carefully noted. By seven
o'clock, I neared the point where I had spotted Cloud and the band.
Custer, a bay roan band stallion, and his bay mare and colt stared at
me as I got quietly out of the car and stuffed my pack with a few essentials: water, an apple, some
cheese, my still camera, and a rain jacket.

The small band went back to grazing as I walked uphill and looked around. I could not see
Cloud and his family. They could have moved into any of the forested canyons that separate each
ridge. I had so little light left, and I really had no idea which way they might have gone. So, as I
often do, I let my feet make the decision. They
led me west, downslope toward Cloud's typical
wintering area between the top of Sykes Ridge
and Big Coulee. I hiked through a deep, wooded
ravine. *So quiet down here*, I thought, *a good place
for a cat to hang out.* I watched for tracks or a
cached victim. Mountain lions cover their kills
with sticks and leaves. I had found the remains of
a cached deer a few years ago, not far from here.

The scolding rattle of a pine squirrel in a
Douglas fir directly over my head startled
me. Happily, I climbed out of the dark ravine
and into the last minutes of sunlight. When I
crested the top of the next ridge, I found what I
was searching for. Cloud looked up, and I waved
as I always do. *Hello, Beautiful.* He went back to
grazing near Flint, Dancer and the mares … and
the two new foals. The little sorrel filly looked
to be about a week old. She was fine-boned with
a delicate star. The dark foal slept, and I moved

*The little sorrel filly looked
to be about a week old.*

33

Two foals, two chances, I thought. Maybe this year they will survive.

closer and sat down, getting out my "dinner" of apple and cheese. *Two foals, two chances, I thought. Maybe this year they will survive.*

The wind, so brisk earlier in the day, died with the setting sun. Nearby, a red-breasted nuthatch called, and I heard a response in the distance. Then the dark foal got up, and I thought "she" was a "he" for a while. *What a stout little girl.* All of Sitka's babies have been sturdy: Custer, Mescalero, Adona, Flint, Dancer, this little one and others I never knew. I was confident she would roan out in time, if she lived long enough.

As I went to bed in the back of my SUV, I could see Custer and his mare and their burly colt through the front windshield. *See you tomorrow,* I whispered … and thought, *lucky me.*

The next day the wind picked up again. A snow-rain mixture fell intermittently. Cloud and his family moved to a sheltered slope on the east side of Sykes Ridge. Thousands of feet below, the Bighorn River meandered through its spectacular canyon. The orange filly was curious—wandering about and rubbing on sticks, nibbling on plants and exploring—while Cloud courted and bred her mother. Velvet had come into her foal heat.

In the morning, low clouds draped the mountaintop and the meadows as I left to begin the long drive home to Colorado. From the highway, I looked back at the distant, flat-topped Arrowheads blanketed with a coat of new snow.

Low clouds draped the mountain when I left.

Chapter 5

Meddling with Nature

Summer came again ... kind of. I returned to find a half-foot of snow on the mountaintop. Since driving was impossible, I started hiking to the teacup bowl. It was tough going, but I kept reminding myself how great the grazing would be after years of below normal moisture. I spotted the beefy, dun stallion Looking Glass in the limber pines. Shaking his head and glaring, he is one of the few horses who acts annoyed with me. I have always respected his wishes, giving him a wide berth at all times.

At the edge of the bowl, I looked down into the lovely round meadow below. It was empty. But, in the distant meadows, framed by angry clouds that enshrouded the Bighorns, dark spots shifted across the snow. Glassing, I saw a pale horse within a band. It was Cloud's mother, the palomino mare, with her family. She is what I call a signature animal. Identify her and you identify the band. Many wild horse families have an unusual member who signals the identity of the entire group. Of course, another great example is Cloud.

Over the next few days, I hiked the area and finally found Cloud and the band not 50 yards from the spot where I'd seen Looking Glass. Velvet and Sitka's foals had grown. I made a point of not naming the little fillies as a way of protecting myself. If mountain lions were to kill them, I hoped that keeping the identities anonymous would diminish the sting of their loss.

The Black had failed to have a foal again this year.

The Black and Aztec, now four and five years of age, failed to produce offspring this year even though the infertility drug, PZP, had been developed as a one-year-only contraceptive. However, three years after receiving it, these young mares had yet to foal. Once again, BLM's flawed management tactics were backfiring. *Why didn't the government leave well enough alone?* I wondered. Natural selection by mountain lions had been successful. The herd was averaging zero population growth due to predation. So, why meddle with nature?

By August, a time when the range should be golden brown, the grass was still green due to a continuing abundance of moisture. Cloud and his family were flourishing and his two little daughters were constant companions, lying side by side like sunbathers on a beach. They groomed each other frequently in those places only reachable with the help of a friend.

Flint was maturing before my eyes. He reminded me of a body builder. What he lacked in height, he made up for in strength. I could see the muscle definition under his coat of dappled gray. He continued to act like his stepfather's lieutenant stallion and Cloud's first line of defense when bachelors came near. I could tell that he relished the opportunity to challenge even the biggest of the bachelors. And, on one occasion, he held his ground against his formidable father, Shaman. *Impressive.* Though cocky and belligerent to other males, Flint was polite to Cloud, mouthing to him like an obedient foal. I marveled at their close relationship and wondered if it would always be this way.

By September, the range had dried out, but the horses were flourishing. Although

Flint was polite to Cloud, mouthing to him like an obedient foal.

Cloud's two little daughters were constant companions

there are natural springs farther out in the Custer National Forest, the only water in the immediate area is the spring-fed water hole, and that is where I camped. As I waited patiently, band after band trailed in.

Each family emerged over the hilltop above the water hole, walking in an orderly single file procession. Once they started downhill, adults and young alike joyfully broke ranks, running wildly to the water with the foals bucking excitedly. Nearly every baby had survived the summer. It was wonderful to see these lively spirits, but also perplexing. *Why had so many survived?*

My mind wandered back to a conversation in June with a mountain lion hunter. He bragged of killing an adult male, tracking the big cat with his dogs for nearly 24 hours in the snow the winter before. I can hardly imagine the terror this elusive predator must have felt. The cat made the fatal mistake of leaping into a tree, allowing the hunter to shoot him off his perch. Three mountain lions in all were killed. *How foolish to kill the very animal that offers a natural way to maintain a herd balance,* I reasoned. As a result of the mountain lion kills, fewer foals died, and the BLM began formulating new methods for removing horses from their home.

Late in the day, two-year-old Dancer wandered off to be bred by Prince. The next day, Cloud's brother Diamond bred the small filly repeatedly and I expected her to go off with him. Typically, a two or three-year-old filly will investigate other stallions, select a mate, and leave her band. But that evening when I watched Cloud's family coming to water, Dancer accompanied them, apparently unwilling to break her familial ties.

Bolder was still with Shaman and his mother. He grazed just feet away from Texas, and when they went to the cool of a shady cluster of firs, he stood quietly by her side. On my return to Colorado, I had an email from the BLM boasting that PZP is reversible. They included a picture of the dun filly in Shaman's band and her newborn. Texas had foaled!

Her filly was a dun, fathered by Shaman. He must have bred Texas the September before when the infertility drug had worn off. The BLM gave her the drug as a yearling and as a two-year-old. And at five, she had given birth to this out-of-season foal. I named the filly, Autumn, for her untimely birth. Texas would nurse her through the cold of winter when there was little to eat. This would put a tremendous drain on the mare's resources and both could die. Still, I was hopeful. *Perhaps the two will have a chance ... if the coming winter is mild.*

Adults and young alike ran wildly to the water.

Diamond courted Dancer and bred her repeatedly.

Chapter 6

Cycles of Life and Death

ate in October, I returned for what would prove to be my last visit of the year. It was a bittersweet journey and one I will never forget. The weather was unsettled. Clouds clustered in dark waves, sailing over the mountaintop, dissolving before they touched the ground, only to build up above the ridgeline.

Two-thirds of the way up Tillett Ridge I stopped to glass west to an isolated island. I always hoped to see a mountain lion sunning in front of one of the many caves on the cliff face. I had come to realize how important the big cats were in keeping a natural balance between predator and their elegant prey.

Atop the mountain, the golden meadows of the Arrowheads spread out before me. Patches of snow lingered from a recent storm and in the distance, I could see the Bighorns still socked in with clouds. Horses grazed in the fields near Penn's Cabin and I excitedly traveled to the little cabin to get a closer look. The haunting, unforgettable cries of stallions sparring came from just over the hill. I hurried to find out who was fighting.

I crested the hill and looked down at black bachelors, a rowdy group of four coal-black males sparring. Surely, their noisy play would draw the attention of any band stallion in the vicinity. No sooner had my thoughts formulated than a pale head appeared over the rise – first the ears, then the face of the unmistakably sculpted head. Cloud was coming.

He was in the lead as his group passed near the bachelors. I watched Sitka and Velvet, then Cloud Dancer, Aztec and The Black; and in the rear were Velvet's pale orange daughter and Flint. I waited to see Sitka's blue roan foal. Several minutes passed and I stared at the rise, expecting the blue roan to come running to catch up with her family. Maybe she had just fallen asleep in the sun, away from the biting wind. But she never came back. I have cried for her many times, and I prayed that her premature loss served a useful purpose – contributing to the natural cycle of life and death. Nature has a plan for its children of the wild, including mustang babies. A foal born wild is privileged, but risks come with freedom. Death may come suddenly on silent feet. Life may be short but blessed. She was one of only a few foals to die that year.

When Flint burst away from the rest of the family, dashing at the bachelors, he took my mind temporarily off the little filly. Despite Flint's small size, he had become a bold young stallion and a terrific fighter. He had learned his lessons well, deflecting bites and kicks from the four bachelors. Cloud was itching to join in and broke into a fluid gallop, changing leads on the uneven ground, modeling the grace of his father, Raven. Cloud's elegant black father lost his band the previous summer as the result of a serious hip injury probably sustained when trying to defend his family. I hoped he might recover his health … and his mares.

Despite Flint's small size, he had become a bold young stallion and a terrific fighter.

Cloud rushed in to challenge one of the blacks. Together, he and Flint made a formidable team, and I did not doubt their ability to deflect even the most determined bachelor or band

stallion. Apparently confident in their power, the family had begun grazing farther away from the other bands. In fact, all the bands seemed to be spreading more apart. With predation waning, the horses appeared to be lapsing once again into complacency, seemingly indifferent to potential threats. *Would it take the near wipeout of the entire foal crop to renew their survival instincts?*

Several inches of snow fell overnight. The next morning, when I started hiking at the edge of the limber pine forest, I saw the tracks of horses in the wet snow. They led into the trees and I followed. Tiny hoof prints intermingled with adult tracks, revealing the presence of a small foal in the group. In an opening, I spotted Bolder who stood near Texas and little Autumn. The golden-colored foal looked frail. Shoulder blades poked out of her thin frame. *She will have trouble surviving,* I worried.

Bolder tried to graze closer to Texas, but she kept him at a distance, away from her daughter. The mare looked lean. Bolder, on the other hand, looked plump with a tubby belly—just the right body condition to survive the winter. When Shaman moved in, Bolder retreated to the perimeter of the band, watching Texas longingly.

Cloud's family wandered into the wet forest giving Bolder and Flint a chance to play. The four-year-olds seemed content to pretend they were band stallions, rearing and spinning, biting teasingly at each other's legs. Playtime ended with each young stallion returning to his band. *When would the desire to start their own families take over?* When Cloud was their age, he dogged the burly band stallion Mateo all summer long, trying to win a mare.

I sat 100 feet or so from Cloud in the afternoon. The family paid no attention to me as they munched snow under the limber pines at the meadow's edge. Both Flint and Cloud looked robust. So did Sitka and the others. Velvet's little filly was apple-butted and strong, and something told me she would survive. I named her Firestorm.

Over the coming months, I saw Cloud's band only once. Even though it was a relatively mild

The four-year-olds seemed content to pretend they were band stallions.

winter, they had chosen to graze in the desert on snow-free flats east of the red buttes. The forage was meager here, but the horses did not need to expend their energy digging through snow. Flint grazed near Aztec. Thankfully, Firestorm was alive and had grown lighter in color. White hairs mixed with orange ones to create an unusual roan coloration. Cloud looked lovely in his pristine pale coat and all the mares were in good flesh. *So far, so good*, I whispered.

When I hiked to the top of a flat mesa above Cloud's family, I spotted Shaman and his band foraging at the edge of Big Coulee where it flattens out into a sandy draw—a far cry from the deep, impassable canyon it becomes only a few miles from here. As I neared the band, I could see Bolder standing near Texas and her foal. Little Autumn looked as if she had actually picked up weight while her mother had lost some. Bolder's black mother Pococeno looked a bit lean also, but she had a light build anyway. Shaman looked wonderful. What a remarkable stallion! He must be nearing twenty, but still powerful.

Late in the afternoon, I hiked back through a meandering canyon, following the tracks of horses in the sandy, red soil. A cottontail bolted from under a blue-green sage and dashed off. I noticed a dark-brown bird atop a butte. Through my binoculars, I could see the golden eagle, his coppery- colored head feathers glowing in the late light. The big bird lifted effortlessly off his rock when I approached; two big wing beats and he was gone. I wished I could soar with him over the desert. *What a view he must have,* I jealously thought. The sun dipped behind the snow-clogged Beartooth Mountains to the northwest just as I reached my car.

Cloud looked lovely in his pristine pale coat.   *Firestorm was alive and had become an unusual roan color.*

While Texas seemed thinner, her little daughter looked like she had picked up weight.

45

Shaman was nearing twenty but still a powerful stallion.

Chapter 7

Dusty's First Day

When I watched Cloud breed Velvet in late May of 2005, I wrote the date in my field notes. Eleven months and 21 days later, I traveled to the Arrowheads hoping the beautiful blue roan mare might have given birth. If 2006 were like 2005, Sitka would foal a few days after Velvet. I imagined two Cloud foals again playing atop their wilderness home.

By the time I arrived at tiny Penn's Cabin atop the mountain, it was late in the afternoon. I dutifully carried a few supplies into the cabin before abandoning these mundane tasks to pursue more exciting adventures. I eagerly hiked up the hill in front of the cabin.

From the rise, I caught sight of horses. Shaman was chasing arthritic Bigfoot away. The dark bay stallion, now around twenty, could still run fast enough to get away from Shaman even though his front knees were the size of soccer balls. Cedar, Shaman's grulla mare, had a new foal. And she was probably coming into her foal heat. Crippled as he was, hopeful Bigfoot was dogging the band, looking for an opportunity to steal Cedar away somehow.

Suddenly, it struck me. Bolder was not with the band! I glassed the edges of the limber pines expecting to see him stride out. Instead, Cloud and his family walked out of the trees and across the

When I watched Cloud breed Velvet in late May, I wrote the date in my field notes.

greening meadow above Shaman's family. Flint was not with Cloud either. *Had both young stallions finally become bachelors? Or, were they just playing over the hill?*

I studied the surrounding slopes as shadows crept up their sides. When I looked back to Cloud's band, I realized that Sitka, too, was gone. *Had she left to foal?* I was confident she had not been stolen. I knew of no stallion strong enough to hold her against her will, and I didn't think she would leave Cloud. *Did the bulge in her flank, which appeared years before, finally affect her ability to give birth? Might she have died while foaling?* I was distressed by a flood of troubling questions and emotions. For five years, she had been Cloud's strong and trusted companion, and the family's anchor.

I focused on the remaining band members. Velvet and Firestorm grazed near Cloud. Velvet's robust daughter, whom I had named The Black, grazed with Aztec. Neither looked pregnant. *How discouraging*, I thought. And I was disappointed that Velvet also showed no signs of being pregnant. If I were right, there would be no Cloud foals this year.

I kept glassing the area somehow expecting Sitka to appear with her foal. After sunset, I watched Cloud snake the band away. With Velvet in the lead, they moved out toward the teacup bowl. I followed them to the bowl and glassed the forest margins. Not seeing Sitka and the young stallions, I resigned myself to the mare's likely death, but welcomed the probability that Bolder and Flint had finally joined the ranks of the bachelors.

The next morning, before sunrise, I got

When I looked back to Cloud's band, I realized Sitka was gone.

It was Velvet, and she had a new foal!

up and hurriedly threw my clothes on, put my camera into the car, grabbed a granola bar and water, and drove away from the cabin. *What was my rush?* I have no idea why I began to search for Cloud's family before I even brushed my teeth or combed my hair.

I drove to the teacup bowl. Seeing no horses there, I drove on and crested a small rise. I could see a horse licking something dark and shiny on the ground. It was Velvet and she had a new foal! I didn't even think she was pregnant. As quickly and quietly as I could, I got the camera and tripod from the car, walked nearer and began filming. It was the first time in 12 years that I had been present during the first moments of a foal's life. I was not the only one to observe the

newborn. In the nearby limber pines, Velvet's family stood watch. The mare had given birth surrounded by her family. Cloud and the mares glanced over from time to time as they grazed or wandered to a snowbank to grab a bite of snow.

As the sun rose higher, Velvet continued to lick the foal who tried to stand only to crumple over at her feet. Then, she ate the slimy birth sack that had encased her baby. Next, she started on the bloody, protein-rich afterbirth. Moments later, there was nothing left. Velvet had destroyed the evidence of the birth, which could have attracted predators.

Just beyond the band, mule deer watched the newborn foal.

Velvet turned once again to lick the face of the foal. He wasn't really as dark as I first thought. As his coat began to dry, I could see he was a pale buckskin like Cloud's grandmother. Native people called this color claybank because it resembled

The sun shone on his dusty-colored coat.

the pale shades of the nearby riverbanks. Only the wife of the chief would be allowed to ride a horse of this sacred color.

The foal tried to get up again and tumbled down. He just couldn't control those long, rickety legs. Velvet lay down right next to him. When the foal tried to get up again and began to tumble backward, Velvet's body was there to steady him. As he stood on trembling legs, surrounded by his family on this wonderfully warm May morning, I could see he was a boy.

Just beyond the band, mule deer wandered around snowdrifts under the limber pines. Flocks of mountain bluebirds lit in the trees, only to flitter off seconds later. Marmots dashed around from rock to rock, stopping to nibble blades of grass. But the colt only paid attention to his mother, looking up at her through bleary eyes. Hunger motivated him to begin searching for the warm liquid that would allow him to survive. *But where did that elusive liquid live?* He probed Velvet's neck and legs. Finally, he worked his way back to her udder and began to nurse. It was critical that he got this first milk called colostrum. It is full of antibodies that would allow the colt to combat disease and infection.

In time, Velvet led her foal to a big, sunny snowbank, and he shakily followed, weaving like a staggering drunk. They joined the rest of the family, and Velvet quenched her thirst on huge,

I planned to follow Dusty through the seasons of his life, as I had Cloud.

sloppy mouthfuls of melting snow. Cloud was a few yards to Dusty's right. The two stared at each other. When Cloud stepped over and tried to sniff him, Velvet laid her ears back, but Cloud softly sniffed the colt's back before she led him away toward the pines. The sun shone brightly on his pale coat. He was a dusty-colored colt. "Dusty," I whispered.

Late in the afternoon, Cloud asked the family to travel uphill a bit. They stopped above the bowl on open slopes near the top of the mountain. Dusty tottered along with his mother, glued to her side. Both lay down together, napping while the rest of the band grazed. As the sun set, I sat quietly watching the mare and foal and the densely forested canyon and cliffs of Cloud's Island beyond them. Snow still clung to the rocky sides of the Island and was piled high under the trees. In the distance, the jagged, snow-covered Beartooth Mountains shone brightly as if lit from within.

Then I noticed that Dusty was up, walking around his sleeping mother. He jumped a few inches off the ground, testing out his legs. He walked stiff-legged to Velvet's head, touched her ears with his nose, and excitedly trotted around her. *What a beautiful colt*, I thought. I love all horses and every color is beautiful, but I have to admit that this pale buckskin shade is my favorite. I imagined that, in time, Dusty's pale legs would turn black to his knees. His black mane and tail would grow long, and the contrast with his buckskin body would be so striking. I planned to follow him through the seasons of his life as I had Cloud.

Hour by hour Dusty was growing stronger.

Velvet got up, breaking my daydream. She stood still, lifted her back leg and placed it behind her to make it easier for Dusty to nurse. His kinky little bush of a tail was crooked, bent to one side just the way it had lain when he was stuffed in Velvet's womb. He flicked it up and down like a pump handle as he suckled enthusiastically. Velvet waited until Dusty was finished, then they joined the family.

As the light faded and the temperature dropped, Dusty began to dance, making unsteady little dashes that ended with herky-jerky stops and hops. I laughed when he leapt into the air, nearly throwing himself over. Hour by hour, he was growing stronger, and I felt very lucky to be part of his first day of life. When it got dark, I reluctantly left the band and returned to Penn's Cabin.

The next morning, I packed up my car and went off to find Dusty, Velvet, and the band. They were in the same area as the night before. As I filmed the colt, he looked toward me. I could tell that he was probably seeing me for the first time, and I waved, hoping he would remember this gesture from a human who meant him no harm. "Stay safe little boy," I whispered, packed up my camera gear, and drove down the mountain.

When it got dark, I reluctantly left Velvet and Dusty.

53

Velvet had put on weight, and Dusty had grown into a sturdy colt.

Chapter 8

The Buckskin Colt

*Cloud would breed
The Black and Aztec,
but a month later both
young mares would
come into heat again.*

May passed into June, and I could hardly wait to return to the Arrowheads. On my first morning back on the mountaintop, I found Cloud's band in the limber pines just below the teacup bowl.

Velvet had put on weight and Dusty had grown into a sturdy colt, especially burly compared to Firestorm who was so feminine. Dusty's half-sister, The Black, grazed near the colt, and I wondered if he might one day match her considerable size. She was huge compared to the other mares. And like Aztec, she continued to come into heat monthly. Cloud would court and breed both mares, but they would come into heat again a month later; and the courting-breeding cycle would continue due to the infertility drugs given to them years before. Even little Dusty responded to the young mares' heat cycles, lifting his upper lip and inhaling as he had seen his father do.

In response to the constant heat cycles of Aztec and The Black, Cloud closely guarded the mares. When other bands came around, he rushed out, staying on the offensive, attacking band stallions and bachelors alike. The dun bachelor, Shane, came around when Dancer was in heat. I didn't see her try to leave with

Little Dusty lifted his lip and inhaled, imitating his father.

the stallion, but she would have had little chance as Cloud viciously drove him off. Beyond just guarding his mares, I noticed a belligerence about Cloud as he galloped out to chase away horses that were far from his band.

When Cloud lost Sitka the month before, he lost his steady partner. She decided when it was time for the band to go to water, take cover, climb uphill, rest or graze. These were her responsibilities, and although Cloud might protest from time to time, he would always go along. After Sitka vanished, Cloud seemed bewildered. Just as his physical skills were reaching their peak, he lost the one horse who could calm his inherently flamboyant and combative spirit. I hoped that Velvet might step up to fill Sitka's shoes but, so far, she showed little interest in taking on the role of a lead mare. The Black seemed a likely candidate, but without a foal, she didn't have the status that a reproductively successful mare would have. And so, Cloud took on the responsibilities of both lead mare and band stallion.

In the afternoon, Cloud and his family traveled to the snow-fed water hole. On the hill above them, I saw five-year-old Bolder playing with an older bachelor. His play had an edgy power as he sparred with the larger dun. Cloud watched them and I sensed he was itching to join in. When it seemed he could not control himself any longer, he marched out, chin tucked to his chest, exuding masculinity. But when he reared up and struck at Bolder, his son did not back down. On the

Five-year-old Bolder had become a feisty bachelor.

contrary, he stood his ground, striking back and screaming. Cloud sniffed Bolder's flank, then his nose. Their heads jerked apart as they screamed even louder. When Cloud pushed on Bolder, his son pushed back, spun and kicked out.

Cloud returned to the band and I wondered if he was just a bit deflated. His intimidation techniques, so successful with the other stallions, had failed to frighten the five-year-old bachelor. Or, if they had, Bolder had not let on.

Then I saw Flint striding over the hill above them and I smiled. He was buff. Muscles bulged under his grullo coat as he walked confidently toward the two bachelors. Bolder watched him intently and I expected the two friends to greet each other and play as they had through the years, but I was very wrong. Bolder reared up and dove at Flint. Flint parried, but the palomino fiercely bit at his rump. Flint trotted off, calmly retreating to the water hole for a drink.

Bolder grew stronger that summer and his coat began to take on a sooty look, black hairs mixing with his golden ones. Grey hair began to blend into his once snowy white tail. *Was there any link between his changing physical appearance and the intensity of his sparring matches?* I imagine not, but the transformation was striking and interesting to contemplate.

Dusty paid attention to everything around him—his father's interaction with Bolder and the behavior of the bachelors. In this, he was very much like his father. As a foal, Cloud watched his father, Raven, and the other wild horses as they interacted with each other. Though Dusty was attentive to his father, Cloud paid little attention to his son, allowing the colt to do pretty much as he pleased. Dusty loved to explore on his own.

Dusty paid attention to everything, much like his father.

57

*Dusty bugged Firestorm, the
closest in age to him.*

Even pinecones seemed interesting. He sniffed the individual cones, then used the low hanging limbs as a back scratcher. On one cool June day, I filmed him smelling rocks and sampling the wild flowers, nibbling on magenta shooting stars and lupine just beginning to bloom. I don't think he noticed the black bear in the shadows of the limber forest gobbling up wads of green grass.

As an only foal, Dusty entertained himself, but he also bugged the closest one in age to him, Firestorm. Dusty would grab the yearling's tail and pull on her long mane as she walked around. He grabbed her cheeks and bit at her legs even when she tried to sleep. He teased The Black, too, nibbling on her face, and I watched in amazement as he suckled her. I had never seen this before. Of course, she had no milk, yet he tugged on her udder anyway. I began to call The Black, Aunt Black. I think she permitted his behavior because she relished the attention of a baby—Dusty was a substitute for the foal she never had.

Late in the day, Dusty watched Dancer wander off—not to join the bachelor her father had driven away but to breed with the dun band stallion, Prince. Just as she had as a two-year-old, she chose a proven stallion, not a young, untested bachelor and, just as she had the year before, she returned to her family. Her return, while unusual, was not unique. I have seen other three-year-old fillies stay with their family bands, too.

By the time I left the mountain in late June, the meadows had erupted into a sea of purple lupine. Cloud's band grazed in a flower-strewn meadow above the water hole. Dusty grazed a few feet from Cloud and I thought, *What a beautiful father and son.*

*Dusty was a substitute for the
foal The Black never had.*

58

What a beautiful father and son, I thought.

Cloud approached the trap, sniffing the ground and the air.

Chapter 9

The Bait Trap

In August, something strange appeared on the mountaintop. The BLM decided to reduce the number of horses in the herd using a method never tried before on the Arrowheads—bait trapping. I found a metal round pen and a camper trailer parked near a grove of firs above the spring-fed water hole. A bait trapper, contracted by the BLM to capture horses, had placed protein blocks inside the corral.

On their way to and from the water hole, horses cautiously passed the pen, giving it a wide berth. But they could smell something new and different in the enclosure, and they grew increasingly curious. Gradually, the bands surrounded the pen and some hesitantly entered the corral through a metal gate. They nibbled on the tasty, sweet blocks. The bait trapper, hidden inside the camper trailer, triggered the gate and it slammed shut, trapping horses inside. Some were freed, and others were driven into a horse trailer and taken to the bottom of the mountain. These horses would be offered for sale on the internet.

I could see Cloud coming in the distance. As he neared the trap, he eyed the pen and the camper parked next to it. He stared into the windows of the camper. Inside, the swarthy face of the trapper was visible as he peered through the red lenses of his night vision binoculars. Cloud looked away, sniffing the ground and the air. Then he entered the trap with Dancer and the mares. I

Dusty stayed outside the trap, playing with a foal in Duke's band.

waited for the trap to slam shut, but it never did. I learned that the trapper had a list of horses to be removed and that none of Cloud's family were on the list. Little Dusty stayed outside the trap and used the close proximity of the bands to gently play with the foals in other family groups. His mother Velvet stayed outside, too, rolling a protein block from under the bottom rail of the pen with her hoof.

When the camper door creaked open, Cloud burst from the pen ... followed by his frightened band. They raced away and down the hill to the water hole. Once they drank, they walked up the opposite hill into the forest. This would become their pattern over the weeks to follow: eat on the tasty protein blocks in the trap, travel to water, and then

Cloud raced away from the trap followed by his family.

62

They galloped down to the water hole.

graze in the forest clearings. I left the mountain, secure in my belief that they would stay safe.

Over the course of a month, the bait inside the trap lured nearly all the horses who were on top of the mountain. Their addiction to the sweet protein blocks grew, and the horses fought over the bait. Band stallions battled each other for access to the trap with its irresistible treats. While fighting over the blocks, Cloud's brother Diamond was severely injured. He lost his band to another stallion, and his son to the trapper. Nineteen horses in all lost their freedom and their families.

During that fateful month, horses were not the only animals to gather into one small spot on the mountaintop. When I returned two weeks later, the trapper told me what had happened. Mountain lions had followed the horses, drawn to an abundance of prey in one central location. The trapper told me of a vicious thunder and lightning storm with swirling winds that had rolled in after sunset one evening. The storm lasted for hours, and the trapper could hear the screams of the mountain lions. He was afraid to go out of his trailer. The next morning, he walked down to the water hole. In the soft mud beside the water, he found the tracks of an adult lion and her two cubs. Beyond the water hole in the trees, he found Dusty's body.

I returned ten days later in search of Dusty's remains. I saw the tracks of the cats in the mud on the shore of the water hole and headed up the hill where the trapper told me to look.

I wandered for an hour or more, in and out of the groves of clustered firs. Then I spotted a bone at the edge of some small juniper bushes. I knelt down and picked it up. Soft marrow still filled the center of the bone. I cradled it in my hands and put it in my pack. It was all I could find of the foal who

Once they drank, they walked up the opposite hill into the forest.

had stolen my heart. The death of Dusty was the single most devastating event in all my years of tracking the wild horses. I felt I had lost my son.

At sunset, I sat with Velvet and Cloud and the band, grieving with them for the foal I had first seen when he was still a dark lump at the feet of his mother. To my knowledge, Dusty and Cloud's little sister Gemini, a lovely orange filly, were the only foals lost to predation that summer. The lions took her the night after they killed Dusty.

It could not get worse than this, I thought. Except, it did. That winter, west of the horse range in the forest service lands, hunters killed an adult female lion. I was certain it was the mother mountain lion who had killed Dusty and Gemini. I did not blame her for taking advantage of the concentration of prey around the bait trap to feed her babies. The lion, without any fault, simply acted on her survival instinct. But the hunters killed her ... and in doing so, they also doomed the kittens who were dependent on her for food. And so, Dusty and Gemini died for absolutely nothing.

Then, nearly two years after Dusty's death, I heard that the BLM had paid hunters to come into the area to kill the lions. I found this hard to believe and asked the new BLM manager why his predecessors would do such a thing. He said that he knew hunters were encouraged to kill the mountain lions, but he did not know they received money for doing so. He explained why the lions were targeted. In order to continue giving infertility drugs to the mares, the herd needed to increase by at least 5% per year. Because of mountain lion predation, the herd had

experienced zero population growth. Unless something happened, the BLM would be forced to cancel their experimental drug program. Dozens of foals fell prey to the big cats to establish a balance between predator and prey. Then over a four-year period, eight lions were killed by human hunters.

To this day, waves of sadness roll over me whenever I think of Dusty's untimely death. He would never be a big brother, a freewheeling bachelor, or a father. And for some strange reason, my saddest thoughts are of winter. Dusty would never see it snow.

My saddest thoughts are of winter. Dusty would never see it snow.

Had Prince stolen Pococeno from Shaman?

Chapter 10

Winds of Change

The long, sorrowful winter passed. In April, I made the drive from Colorado to the Arrowheads once again. I hoped to see Cloud and his family and Flint and Bolder.

On Tillett ridge, I started hiking just as it began to snow. I spotted Electra, Cloud's lovely red roan sister. She walked out of the grove of Douglas firs just above me. *What a beautiful mare,* I thought. I saw behind her a black mare emerge from the trees. It was Bolder's mother, Pococeno! Then the dun stallion Prince appeared. Although he lost his entire family in 2003, he managed to rebuild a band the following year. Now he had added another mare to his family. *Had Prince stolen Pococeno from Shaman?* I couldn't imagine how he might have managed it. *Maybe the mare left of her own accord?* That seemed more likely—unless something unexpected had happened to Shaman. I had to find out.

The next day I drove up on Sykes, parked above the red buttes, and began hiking across the top of a mesa capped with smooth, slab-like rocks. I named the ridge Indian Mesa. Long ago, the native people used the area. Over the years, arrowpoints have been found here – and even a burial site. It was easy to see why the mesa was popular. To the west, the desert below unfolded from the buttes all the way to the wide mouth of Big Coulee Canyon. Beyond the canyon,

*I found a large, flat rock to sit on,
and set up my spotting scope.*

much of Tillett Ridge was visible sloping uphill to the northwest. And I could see most of lower Sykes Ridge as it paralleled the east side of Big Coulee and rose up to the north.

I found a large, flat rock to sit on, and I set up the spotting scope. I aimed up high on Sykes, methodically scanning each small snowy section at a time. I worked my way down the ridges to their drop-off into Big Coulee. *Horses!* I zoomed in a bit on a grulla, two duns, and a black. It had to be Shaman's mares. A minute later, the dun stallion strode out from behind a juniper. I felt relieved to see him looking fine.

Then another horse appeared from behind the dense bushes. *It was Bolder! Had he come back home again?* The dark palomino walked past Texas and stood in front of Shaman. The two stallions touched noses. Then Bolder did something I had never seen him do before—not to Shaman, anyway. He stomped his foot down sharply right in front of his stepfather. Then he stomped again, shook his head, stared and walked away. Shaman shook his head, too, but did not react to what looked like a challenge to me. Instead, the older stallion went back to grazing with his mares. They gradually drifted out of sight into juniper thickets above the big canyon. Bolder followed them, and I kept looking, but they never reappeared. I stood up, scanning the many canyons that separated me from Shaman's band. The horses might as well have been on the moon, for I was powerless to reach them.

Bolder, looking even darker in color, walked past Texas and stood toe to toe with Shaman.

I sat back down and continued to check out other sections of lower Sykes, hoping to catch a glimpse of Cloud. Instead, I saw Flint all alone. He, too, was miles away … in an inaccessible spot.

After hours staring through the scope with my left eye, I switched to my right eye without

The first-born of the season was a stout bay filly named Halo.

success, and I had to quit. On the way down Sykes, my spirits were lifted with sightings of the season's first-born foals: a stout bay filly I named Halo and a just hours-old grulla filly I named Helena Montana. New life had returned to the Arrowheads.

I named the hours-old filly Helena Montana.

It looked like Shaman, walking with a purpose.

Chapter 11

The Hideout

In mid-May, I returned. I knew the horses would be higher on the ridges, and if I were to find Cloud, Shaman, Bolder and Flint, I would have to drive up Sykes. Swallowing hard, I started up the hideous road, past Indian Mesa, through Cougar Canyon, and up to a spot where I got the first views of the mid-ridges of Sykes. I stopped and saw a lone dun horse wandering on a ridgeline. But he dropped out of sight before I could get a closer look with my scope.

I drove on, hoping to catch another glimpse. I started hiking a ridge near where I thought I had spotted the dun, an area where I had sighted Cloud in seasons past. After an hour or so, I glimpsed a horse atop the ridge to my right, and I whipped my binoculars to my eyes just as he dropped over the far rim. It was the dun. He sure looked like Shaman, and he was not meandering but walking with a purpose. I scanned the area for other horses. The horse appeared to be alone!

Shaman is a legend on the Arrowheads. When I first came to the mountain in 1994, he led a band of sixteen horses. Captured in a BLM roundup that fall, Shaman was nearly sold to a pack trip operator in Cody, Wyoming. But we were able to successfully plead with the BLM for his release. Before they let him go, family members not selected for sale were set free without him, including his lead mare Sitka. So, Shaman had to start building a band all over

Combining power with speed, Shaman was a devastating fighter, yet remarkably gentle.

again. By 1997, he had created a big family once more, including Sitka. She remained his lead mare until Cloud somehow stole her away in 2001. Through the years, Shaman retained his dominant position as a band stallion, along with Cloud's father Raven.

Combining power with speed, Shaman was a devastating fighter. He was fond of charging an opponent at a blinding gallop. To a challenger, it must have been like facing a runaway train on a downhill track. If his rival did not run away like a scared rabbit (as most did), he would stay low and, when the opponent reared up in defense, he would strike them full force in the chest, knocking them over backwards or throwing them off balance. He picked his fights wisely, starting few but finishing them all. Yet, for all this strength, Shaman was remarkably gentle.

Now I believed he was alone, and I thought he was looking for his family. I joined in his search.

I hiked back to the road and started driving very slowly uphill with my windows rolled down, not only looking but listening. I could hear the tap of a woodpecker foraging for insects inside a dead fir tree, the insistent *dee-dee-dee* of a mountain chickadee, and the chatter of a red squirrel. I could see Clark's nutcrackers flying overhead, the large grey, black and white birds landed in tall trees up ahead. I neither saw nor heard a horse.

About a mile and a half before reaching the open meadows atop the mountain, I decided to hike through a sparsely treed side slope with some good, early grazing. Plenty Coups and his family used to frequent the area and I always thought of the elegant blue roan stallion when I passed the spot. *If he and his family liked the area, others would too,* I reasoned. The side slope flattened out and gave way to rocky slabs that dropped sharply into a narrow, forested canyon. I stared into the canyon and across to a steep cliff face and a dense forest just beyond its rocky edge. It was an isolated island below the mountaintop. *Impassable from here,* I concluded.

Looking left, I glassed far down on Sykes and spotted the dun again. He walked, then stopped and stared. It was Shaman. *He is watching and listening, too,* I thought.

I stubbornly returned to stare across the deep canyons at the isolated island. I was sure there were horses there.

The sun dropped behind the western hills, and I hiked back to my camp, disappointed at not finding any wild horse bands.

The next morning, I continued my search. Not locating Shaman or any horses on the visible ridgetops of Sykes, I stubbornly returned to stare across the deep canyon at the isolated island. I was sure there were horses over there. Clark's nutcrackers landed in the trees above my head and cawed sharply before flying off, gliding with ease across the canyon onto trees at the edge of the island. *Easy for you!* I thought jealously. As I walked along the rocky cliff face, I looked up at snow on the mountaintop and wondered if I might be able to drive to Penn's Cabin. I sat down and watched for movement on the island. A faint cry echoed from the forest across the canyon. *A horse ... or maybe, a Nutcracker's call?*

When she was a foal I had named her Cascade for the distinctive marking on her face.

I sat quietly and continued to listen. Hours passed. I ate my peanut butter and jelly sandwich on the sunny cliff face and day dreamed about what this beautiful place might have looked liked a million years ago when it was the shore of a huge lake. A call pierced the air, and I jerked back to reality. The cry was no bird, but a horse. I rushed back to get my heavy camera gear. There was no way to carry it across the canyon, so I had to hope that the horses might show themselves on the cliff edges. I realized it was only a remote possibility and that I was being somewhat irrational, but I was determined to figure out who was over there.

By mid-afternoon, as I sat munching on my apple, I heard branches break across the canyon and focused in on trees with my binoculars. I could see movement! When what looked like a tree trunk moved, I excitedly got up and focused my long lens. It was a slender grullo horse who I thought might be a young bachelor. Then, I saw a black horse, and

Following Bolder was one of Shaman's mares.

when she turned her head, I gasped, recognizing her by the irregular, long white mark on her face. It was Electra's daughter, a filly I had named Cascade for her unusual face marking. She was one of Shaman's mares. I began to film.

The grulla must be the mare I named Cedar years ago when she was just a playful foal. Then I saw a lighter horse walk out of the forest to the edge of the island. It was Bolder! Following him was Texas and her two-year-old daughter, Autumn. Bolder had somehow stolen Shaman's entire family. I noticed something small moving in the trees. A pale dun foal walked out of the forest and began nursing her mother, Cedar. When the mare and foal drifted into the deep shadows of the forest, I watched Bolder follow them. He gently mounted the mare who offered no resistance. *Next May*, I thought, *there might be a Bolder foal on the Arrowheads.*

Bolder had waited to take over the band only after his mother was with another stallion. *Amazing!* And ... how incredibly intelligent it was of him to hide out with his stepfather's family on an isolated island. It gave him time to bond with the mares, not as the little brother they had grown up with, but as their band stallion. I will forever wonder how he stole them. *Did he battle Shaman for the mares, or did he somehow spirit them away in the night?*

As the band disappeared into the forest late in the afternoon, I looked up at the light reflecting off a huge bowl of snow atop the mountain. When the snow melts on their isolated island, the family will have to come to the mountaintop. There will be no place to hide on the wide subalpine meadows. *Will Bolder be strong enough to hang onto all these mares? And what will happen when Shaman shows up?*

Bolder had somehow stolen Shaman's entire family including his grulla mare with a newborn foal.

The next day, I took a chance. Fighting through deep snowdrifts just below the open meadows, I was able to reach the mountaintop. What I saw shocked me!

When the snow melts on their isolated island, the band will have to come to the mountaintop.

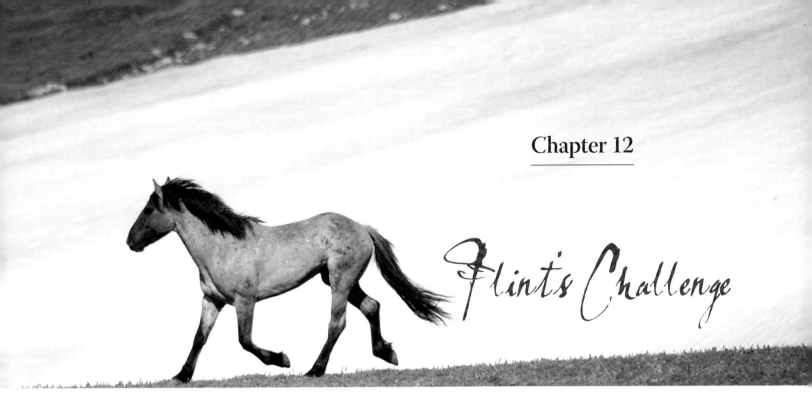

Chapter 12

Flint's Challenge

I noticed Flint following Cloud at a determined trot.

The calls of stallions echoed over the high meadows. The sound was a magnet for me and I started hiking. I reached the hilltop in front of Penn's Cabin and looked west to a giant wall of snow above the water hole and Cloud racing toward me at a dead run. Something was wrong, and I feared he had lost his family. In less than a minute, however, he galloped to his band unchallenged. Then I noticed Flint following Cloud at a determined trot. The compact, grullo stallion looked like a finely tuned athlete.

As Cloud reached his band, he spun around and glared back at Flint. The grullo slowed down and stopped. He lifted his lip, sniffing the air. He could smell a mare in heat. Then Flint walked toward Cloud and the band. He was about 100 feet from the family when Cloud shook his head in annoyance and stomped his front foot. Flint stopped and began to graze nonchalantly. The tactic was not new to me.

When Cloud was only four, he dogged the band stallion Mateo and his family day and night in hopes of winning his grulla mare. Cloud would move toward the band, taking a bite of grass, and then he would walk closer as if he had no interest in them at all. When some kind of invisible barrier was broken, Mateo would charge out after him. This dangerous game of tag went on for months with Cloud finally giving up after he lost 100 pounds or more … and went lame.

Even though Flint ran far away, Cloud pursued him relentlessly.

For Flint to try this tactic with Cloud was unthinkable. He was always so respectful and obedient, and they were such good friends ... or so I thought. Still, here was Flint inching forward, nibbling at blades of grass. He glanced up, his head just inches above the ground, taking one tiny, slow, half step after another. Suddenly, Cloud burst into a gallop with his ears pinned back racing toward Flint who turned tail, dipping his rear end and tucking his tail like a submissive dog. Even though Flint ran far away, Cloud pursued him relentlessly, chasing him over a distant hill beyond the water hole. I could hear their screams and knew they were fighting.

Meanwhile, Cloud's family grazed away on the protein rich early grasses as if nothing were happening. Minutes passed and I saw Cloud running back to his band. Seconds later, Flint crested the hill, following him at a steady trot.

Was Flint really trying to steal his stepfather's family? After my discovery of Bolder with Shaman's band, nothing should have surprised me. But two stepsons trying to steal their stepfathers' bands at almost the same time—now, what were the odds of this happening? *And would Flint be as successful as Bolder?* Over the next few days, I filmed the cat and mouse game and realized the danger that Cloud faced.

When Santa Fe arrived on the mountaintop with his small family, I didn't think too much about it. The handsome bay stallion has always been one of my favorites, but he is more of a lover than a fighter. He is just Cloud's age, born less than a week earlier in May of 1995, and they were frequent companions as bachelors.

Santa Fe and his family grazed near Cloud. Opposite Santa Fe on the other side of Cloud's band was Flint, who edged closer to the band. If Cloud raced after Flint on one of their long distance chases, Santa Fe could sweep in and try to steal a Cloud mare. Then I noticed Cloud's two-year-

Santa Fe turned and moved in quickly behind Dancer.

old daughter, Firestorm, wander off into trees at the edge of the wide meadow where mule deer were grazing. Cloud trotted over to retrieve the filly, snaking her back. "Let her go," I whispered. No sooner back, she wandered off again … and Cloud went to get her.

With Cloud focused on Firestorm, Santa Fe moved in quickly behind Dancer. The four-year-old was small but feisty like her mother. She kicked at the stallion, slowing him down. Cloud left Firestorm to drive Santa Fe away from Dancer. He knew his old bachelor friend was not much of a challenger, yet he was a band stallion, so he could not be ignored. Seeing Cloud's preoccupation with Santa Fe, Flint walked up to the family. Cloud spotted him, exploding into action, and immediately drove him far away.

This is when Santa Fe returned and went after The Black. When Cloud caught sight of what was going on with his band, he stopped chasing Flint and galloped back to Santa Fe, forcing him away. Cloud's insistence on running Flint far away while tackling Santa Fe's advances was risky. If an aggressive bachelor or a tougher band stallion discovered the situation, it could prove very serious for Cloud. The pale stallion was formidable but not invincible.

The next day, Santa Fe was still hanging around the meadow with his little family. I noticed Firestorm staring at him from time to time and wondered if she was in heat. Santa Fe seemed to have a special gift for attracting young fillies.

I caught a glimpse of Flint slipping into the limber pines behind an enormous snowdrift. Out of the sight of Cloud's family, he stepped behind the trees and stopped, then took one

Cloud stopped chasing Flint and galloped back to Santa Fe, forcing him away.

Flint ran back into the open meadow with an angry Cloud on his heels.

cautious step after another, weaving his way through the pines and onto the drift. From there he could see Firestorm and Dancer, and the mares just on the other side of the snowbank. When Cloud saw a dark object moving on the white drift, he was off like a shot, plunging into the drift, sending the snow flying. Just as quickly, Flint spun around and ran back into the open meadow with an angry Cloud on his heels.

In the distance, I saw Cloud's younger brother, Red Raven, approaching. *This could be trouble,* I thought. Red Raven only had two mares, Blue Sioux and Sitka's daughter, Adona. Both were blue roans. I always thought Red Raven fancied Dancer. I believe that stallions and mares are sometimes drawn to certain colors, and both Cloud and Red Raven seem to fancy blue roans. Horses of this color are sacred to the Navajo people. Maybe they are special to these Raven sons as well.

When Cloud saw Red Raven coming, he wheeled away from Flint and took the offensive, confronting his younger brother. They pawed the air and screamed at each other, but the fight was more ceremonial then serious. After the spat, Cloud moved off and rolled in a small grass-free

When Cloud saw Red Raven coming, he confronted his younger brother.

Cloud shook his head in irritation, frustrated that Flint would not stand and fight.

spot. Minutes later, Red Raven walked to the same spot and rolled. Then, hours later, I watched Flint walk to the identical spot and roll too. *What was going on here?* Years before, I filmed bison bulls in their dirt wallows, rolling and urinating. They were scent marking the wallows, sending a message to other bulls that this was their turf and, perhaps, sending messages about their health and vitality as well. Wild stallions regularly use stud piles to convey these types of messages, but I never realized that they also communicate using these communal rolling places. I did not see them urinate, but they were clearly replacing their scent with that of their predecessors.

Red Raven stayed a comfortable distance away from Cloud's band, but I saw him watching Dancer. Cloud kept an eye on both Red Raven and Santa Fe, but he was most concerned with Flint. *Did he sense the strength of the colt he had raised? Had he taught him too well?* Cloud chased Flint away, shaking his head back and forth in irritation. He wanted the grullo to stand and fight, but Flint's battle tactics did not include volunteering to stand toe-to-toe with Cloud. He opted to wait him out and wear him down.

I watched Flint walk to a little rise. He looked down the valley at other stallions defending their mares, but the young stallion seemed interested only in his stepfather's band. I reluctantly left the mountain to travel home to Colorado, unsure what might happen next. But less than two weeks later, I returned.

Chapter 13

Rain

The end of May was wet and cold with intermittent sleet, snow and rain. As I drove up Tillett Ridge, there was not a horse to be seen— not on the lower ridges, in the forest, or on the open meadows atop the mountain. The horses must have been hiding in the trees because they were nowhere to be seen.

The next morning, I drove down on Sykes, out of the sleet and into a light, cold drizzle. Fog drifted silently around craggy rock spires and rolled in waves over the edge of Sykes Ridge and into the Bighorn Canyon. It was strange to be in a wild horse range and see no wild horses, as if they had gone on vacation to a warmer place. Then I saw movement in the forest. A horse was traveling downhill on a trail through the Douglas firs. When he walked through a clearing, I could see it was Flint! He was all alone and walking with a purpose. *Was Cloud nearby?*

I glassed around quickly but saw nothing—just Flint marching down the mountain. At the drop-off into Cougar Canyon, he stopped and looked around in the fog and rain. I wasn't sure if he was searching for Cloud's family or just looking for any mare to capture. Then he disappeared on switchbacks into the canyon. I decided to let him go. Cloud would not be this far down the mountain. At least, I didn't think so.

Velvet and her newborn moved nervously away, unable to find shelter from the driving sleet.

I drove back up Sykes at a crawl, stopping and glassing often. Hoping to see Bolder and the mares again, I hiked out to the cliff face across from their island hideout. *Were they still hiding out there?* It was eerily quiet, save for the *drip-drip-drip* of the rain falling off tree limbs onto the rocks at the cliff edge.

The next day was soggier still, far too wet to drive anywhere, and I spent most of the day looking out of the door of Penn's Cabin into the sleet and fog. But I did venture out for a short, blustery walk when I saw Mescalero and his family appear with their new foal. The young band stallion was Flint's full brother, another Sitka and Shaman son. Mescalero's black mare had given birth to a lightly built red filly. Mother and daughter stood on the sheltered side of a thick stand of firs above the snow-fed water hole. They were wet but out of the wind. *How tough these horses are*, I thought, as I wimped out and hustled back to the cabin.

The next day was wet, too, but I took a chance and started down Tillett in the mud. I saw horses just past the teacup bowl. The husky, dun stallion Looking Glass and his family of mares and yearlings stood huddled together under the firs, soaked to the bone. When I nearly slid off the road, I lost my nerve, parked, and began hiking. I was glad I did.

A muffled *woo ... woo-woo-woo* echoed through the waterlogged forest. I recognized the call and

Through the trees, mule deer watched Cloud's family in the fog.

hiked to find a male blue grouse on a snowdrift in the fog, booming for a mate. As he called, he flared the feathers on his neck to expose a round patch of bright red, fleshy skin called a gular sac. As I walked away, I could still here him booming, and I hoped he would succeed in finding a female.

Through the trees, I saw mule deer grazing and just beyond them, horses. It was Cloud and his family in a wet, windy clearing. Dancer walked up to Aztec and the Black, lifting her upper lip as if protesting the hideous weather. Firestorm grazed a bit farther away near Cloud who calmly munched on the moisture-laden grass. What a switch from a few weeks ago when he was on high alert and poised for battle. *Did the family come down here to get out of the worst of the weather or were they hiding from Flint?*

Then, I caught sight of Velvet and a newborn foal. As I worked my way around the band to get closer, the mule deer paid little

A male blue grouse stood on a snowdrift booming for a mate.

attention but Velvet seemed nervous. I waved to let her know it was me, but she was still leery and moved a short distance away with the dark brown foal tottering at her side. I stepped back and watched from under a limber pine. The foal was a tall and slender filly. She reminded me of her mother as a youngster—feminine and Spanish looking.

The horses of the Arrowheads are genetically unique, the direct descendents of the horses of the Conquistadors. Five hundred years ago the Spanish set up horse breeding farms in the Caribbean. The horses were essential to the conquest of Mexico and South America. The sleet-drenched foal in the soggy forest was a perfect example of the ideal Spanish horse. She had a short back, a low tail setting, and a beautifully tapered head that ended with a tiny, teacup nose.

Rain is what I'll call you little girl.

85

I spotted Cloud's family in a grove of trees above Big Coulee.

Chapter 14

After the Storm

Finally, the weather cleared and I hiked back where I had discovered Rain two days before. There were horses in the limber pines, but not the ones I hoped to find. *Where are you, Cloud?*

From the top of Tillett, I started glassing down on the ridges of Sykes, and then I panned over to Tillett Ridge and saw horses. They had wisely retreated from the frigid heights to the lower ridges. I headed down, hoping to find Cloud's band and little Rain.

I smiled as I passed band after band. Some were drinking and playing in puddles right in the road. Often, wild horses could be impossible to find, and then quite unexpectedly, dozens could be seen with ease. *Feast or famine*, I thought.

As I watched the horses having fun and basking in the warm sun, I spotted Cloud's family behind a grove of trees above the Bighorn Canyon. They moved into the clear and I saw Aztec, Dancer, The Black, Firestorm, Cloud, and then Velvet in the shadow of a tree, but not Rain. Maybe she was sleeping, lying flat in the grass. My heart dropped when I circled them and didn't see her. I moved even closer as Cloud walked up to Velvet, making a soft, guttural, huffing sound. The mare was coming into heat, and he was sweet talking her. Suddenly, a dark head popped up in the shadows at their feet. *Rain!* The filly sprang up,

Rain's dark brown coat was the color of a mink and looked every bit as soft.

and like a ballerina warming up for a dance, she stretched out one of her long tapered back legs and pointed her toe. She nursed her mother, and then walked into the sun. *What a beauty.* Her dark brown coat was the color of a mink and looked every bit as soft. How different she was from Dusty in color and in build. *Wouldn't he have loved to show his little sister around?*

The band started to move out, walking through the low blue green sage, the scent of it filling the air. *What a glorious smell*, I thought. Beyond the band was Big Coulee, and beyond the huge canyon was Sykes Ridge. I took out my binoculars and scanned across the many fingers of open meadows divided by timbered canyons, hoping to see Flint. I looked closely at the area on Sykes where the road dropped into Cougar Canyon, the last place I had seen him days before, but I saw no horses.

Near the Sykes edge of Big Coulee, a flat island dropped gradually and then precipitously into the canyon. I had seen Mateo and Electra there in years past, before she was stolen away by Prince. I called it Mateo's Island, in honor of the stocky bay stallion. There was movement on the island—a lone black horse was walking downhill toward the end of the island where it drops into the canyon.

I hiked closer to the edge of Big Coulee and sat on a rock, watching. The black horse stopped to take a bite or two of grass and then walked on. He was a stallion, and from the pace of his walk, he was clearly on a mission. When I panned to his right, I found the object of his attention—Bolder, the mares, and Cedar's little foal. Like the bands on Tillett, they also descended to avoid the worst of the weather. In doing so, they exposed themselves to this black stallion. *Who was he?* I asked myself.

I set up my scope to get a closer look and recognized his tall, lean build and his tiny star.

The tough bachelor,
Bo, was stalking Bolder
and his family.

I have known him all his life. He was Bo, the son of Boomer and the sorrel mare Coppertop, two lovely horses that had died several years before. Bo was older than Bolder and a tough bachelor. I imagined he would test the young palomino … if he hadn't already.

Bolder's mares and the foal followed a trail that dropped off the edge of the Island. When Bolder stopped and looked almost nonchalantly at the black bachelor, Bo stopped, too. *Was the older stallion hesitant to take on the younger palomino?* Bolder followed his mares, but stopped once again and looked back at Bo who froze. Bolder walked on, joining the mares as they calmly dropped out of sight. I watched Bo follow.

I hustled to my right, trying to see them as they descended into the canyon. *Where were they going anyway?* Big Coulee is deep, with shear drop-offs. It is impassable … or so I thought. Unable to get a view of the horses, I reluctantly left the canyon edge to rejoin Cloud and his family as they moved slowly toward the mountaintop.

The next day, I found Cloud, Rain and her mother Velvet, and the rest of the family in the limber pines, within a quarter mile from where the little filly had been born. What a difference a few days made. It was wonderfully warm with just the hint of a breeze.

Rain and Velvet and the band were working their way up Tillett Ridge.

89

I watched Rain staring intently into the trees and followed her line of sight into the limber pines. A black bear was gorging on big mouthfuls of new green grass growing in profusion under the open canopy of the pines. I quietly began filming. Then I saw a tiny bear cub climbing the tree behind its mother. Up and up the little bear scrambled, joining his cinnamon-colored twin, where they sat together on a lichen-covered limb. The two stared innocently back at me.

Suddenly, I heard a noise. *Hoofbeats!* I panned my camera 180 degrees to see Bolder and his family hustling up the mountain. *They had somehow crossed Big Coulee ... but how?* Cloud heard them, too, and trotted out to watch them pass – but made no move to chase his son.

Now, the fireworks will begin, I thought. Over 100 horses will be in the high meadows, and a young, first-time band stallion like Bolder with four mares and a foal will be tested. *Could Cloud's young son hold up to this kind of intense pressure?* The answer would surprise me!

90

Chapter 15

Fathers and Sons

A dozen bands or more roamed the high meadows below Penn's cabin.

ran as fast as I could with my camera, struggling to catch up with the band. Bolder, the mares and the foal were already in the teacup bowl by the time I could set up on the cliffs above. Bo, whom I expected to see challenging Bolder, was nowhere to be seen. Instead, new bachelors far older than Bolder had flanked his family. The dun stallion, Sandman, raced on their left. The red roan, Chance, galloped on their right. Bolder did not go for either one. Rather, he pulled up the rear with Cascade in the lead. She led the family at a gallop across the open bowl and up the far hillside, fearlessly mounting the hill with her family close behind. The trotting band looked like a finely tuned military unit marching in quickstep up the steep hill that separated the bowl from the open meadows atop the mountain.

Only when Sandman and Chance charged at Bolder from the same side did the palomino react. He darted out fiercely, ears pinned to his golden head. The two bachelors reversed course in unison. "Wow!" I whispered in disbelief. Without wasting any effort, Bolder rejoined the mares as they reached the hilltop and disappeared. I believed that trouble waited just over the hill. A dozen or more wild horse bands could be on the other side.

By the time I got over the mountain, Bolder was already near Penn's cabin. Prince stood at attention with Electra, Pococeno (Bolder's mother), and the

By the time I could get around the mountain, Bolder and his family were already beyond the cabin.

rest of his family. He was battle-tested and looked terrific, his dun coat shining reddish gold in the sunlight. Prince glared at Bolder.

Perhaps the young palomino sensed the challenge in Prince's glinty gaze for he marched up to him. They touched noses. I could hear their heavy breathing, inhaling the essence of each other. Then they screamed! Their heads flew back and they struck out with their front legs. Bolder did not back down. Instead, he calmly turned his back on Prince and walked to his mares as if he had been performing these age-old band stallion rituals for years. Prince respectfully watched the youngster leave. I was beyond surprised.

Then I saw horses coming over the distant hill above the teacup bowl. It was Cloud and his family with Rain. The little filly flew past Velvet on the slender legs of a born runner. The band raced toward Penn's Cabin.

Perhaps the young palomino sensed the challenge in Prince's glinty gaze.

To the east of the cabin, Flint strode confidently uphill. Cathedral spires jutted up dramatically behind him. He stopped when he saw Cloud and the family coming. But when Cloud spotted him standing a half mile away, he raced across the meadow at top speed. There was no ritual sniffing; rather, Cloud and Flint screamed, swirled, stomped, reared and postured. Flint unexpectedly whipped around and landed a kick to Cloud's side and trotted off. I anticipated that Cloud would finish the fight. Instead, he returned to his family at a gallop, driving them far below the cabin to the edge of the limber pine forest. I have never seen a horse that could push Cloud's buttons as consistently as Flint.

The young grullo did not follow the band; rather, he walked forward a few steps and watched, the snowy Bighorn Mountains gleaming behind him. Flint had bulked up even more, his muscle definition impressive under his compact, grayish form. As I watched him stare at the father who raised him, I wondered what was going on in his head. *Does he really want to steal Cloud's band, or does he just want to come home?* Regardless of Flint's intentions, Cloud seemed convinced he was a threat and snaked the band even farther away.

The next day dawned warm and sunny. From Penn's Cabin, I could see a horse walking on the distant rim that separated the teacup bowl from the open meadows on top of the mountain. Even without my binoculars, I could see that the lone horse was moving with purpose. Through my glasses, I identified the familiar form of Shaman and glanced back to Bolder. The approaching danger caught Bolder's watchful eye. *From this far away, could Bolder tell it was his stepfather?*

Shaman just kept coming, and I found my chest tighten with expectation. From time to time, he dipped his head just above the new grasses. Like a bloodhound on the scent, he was tracking his family and the young stallion who had stolen them.

Shaman just kept coming, and I felt my chest tighten.

When Shaman neared the band, he slowed his pace. Rather than walking directly at them, he advanced at an angle. Bolder noticed that Cedar's little filly daughter had strayed from the band and quickly trotted out to gently snake her back to her mother and the other mares.

Bolder arched his neck and puffed up, making himself seem taller and bigger. He ran full speed toward Shaman who dodged out of the way and cantered off a few yards. Bolder trotted back to his band and drove them away at a gallop. Shaman turned, and watched. I had never seen him give ground to any stallion—ever. Bolder had just neutralized Shaman's characteristic offensive charge by taking the offensive first.

Then, the familiar dance began. Shaman started to dog the band, hoping to wear the young band stallion down both physically and emotionally. I wondered if Bolder would be able to withstand this kind of relentless pressure from such a savvy stallion. The psychological warfare continued for weeks.

Bolder arched his neck and puffed up, making himself seem taller and bigger.

I named Cloud's granddaughter Arrow for her huge, arrow-shaped star.

Less than a mile away, I found Cloud and his expanded family.

Chapter 16

Courting Firestorm

Bolder and the band grazed quietly above the teacup bowl. Shaman grazed along side the family, looking like the dominant band stallion he had always been. However, looks can be deceiving. I could tell Bolder was in command for he kept himself between Shaman and the mares. When I focused in on the two stallions with my big lens, I could see their battle wounds, clear evidence that fights had taken place during my absence. Bolder had a nasty gash that just missed putting out his eye. Shaman had open wounds— cuts on his leg and jaw. *I figured a final showdown had to take place ... but when?*

Less than a mile away, I found Cloud and his expanded family. Dancer had given birth to a little bay with a huge, arrow-shaped star on her forehead. I named the short but sturdy filly, Arrow. Nearly a year before, Dancer wandered off and was bred by Prince. With Arrow, Cloud became a new grandpa.

Every family needs a clown, and Arrow certainly fit the bill. When the band lay down for a mid-morning nap in a sunny meadow, Arrow refused to follow suit. Instead, she milled around and tried to get her mother up. Dancer simply ignored her, so Arrow bugged the other mares. She tried to nurse The Black who bit at her. Next, Arrow went over and pawed at Velvet who stood up in annoyance. When Arrow tried to nurse her, Velvet laid her ears back and

Every family needs a clown, and Arrow certainly fit the bill.

turned to stare at her. Then Rain stood up and Arrow tried to nurse her! As I filmed, I tried not to jiggle the camera with my quiet laughter.

The next morning, the sun rose into a cloudless sky. I found Cloud's mares grazing in the limber pines just below the teacup bowl. A sudden shriek startled me, and I hiked through the trees to find Cloud and the older bachelor, Sandman. The two were standing on their hind legs striking at each other. This was no playful bout but a serious fight. Sandman, however, was no match for Cloud and he backed away, shaking his head in irritation. *What's this about?* I wondered. Cloud's mares paid no notice, continuing to graze amongst the trees. Rain and Arrow walked at their mothers' sides. That's when I noticed Firestorm was missing and looked around for her.

The two-year-old filly wasn't far off. She was standing in a sunlit opening in the forest with her tail held up a bit. *You're in heat, aren't you girl?* I thought to myself. That was why Sandman was hanging around. And he wasn't the only one! Cloud's daughter was drawing bachelors and band stallions from every direction; even Cloud's father, Raven, lurked among the trees. He had been unable to recover his mares after his injury two years ago ... but not his will to win a female. I noticed another

Cloud and the old bachelor, Sandman, battled in the limber pines.

Even Cloud's father, Raven, was drawn to the scent of the filly.

stallion trotting up. Like Raven, he was black. "Bo," I whispered. He, too, could smell the scent of the filly. The bay band stallion Starman approached, but Cloud was quick to defend his daughter, rearing up and striking at him. Cloud fended them all off and escorted Firestorm back to the family. But within minutes, she wandered off again.

I watched as another stallion joined the crowd of hopeful suitors. It was the handsome band stallion, Santa Fe, who attempted to steal a Cloud mare the year before. He walked into a clearing about 100 feet from Firestorm. The filly and the stallion stared at each other for a long time before Firestorm took a few steps toward him. Then Santa Fe walked hesitantly toward her. Cloud stood in the shade of the pines with the rest of his family, observing the two. Arrow waited by her mother, yawning. I smiled at the tiny filly who seemed truly bored with the situation.

Santa Fe and Firestorm walked up to each other and touched noses. He talked to her in seductive stallion-speak, snuffling softly. Then he sniffed her sides and hips and gently mounted her. Cloud continued to watch, making no move to interfere. *Did he approve of the match?*

After mating, Santa Fe touched the filly's face and walked away. She followed him. They dropped out of sight into the teacup bowl, and I thought I had seen Firestorm make her choice of a mate and was happy for her. A few minutes later, I was surprised to see Cloud dashing away into the bowl. He ran to his daughter and Santa Fe, swiftly driving the stallion away. Then, Cloud snaked Firestorm

Handsome Santa Fe joined the hopeful suitors.

99

back to the family as she mouthed her apology, clacking her teeth together like a submissive foal.

While Santa Fe was seducing Firestorm and trying to win her back, he lost his family to Raven. The beautiful old stallion pranced in proud circles, displaying his dancer's form as he drove the two mares and the foal away. But his theft was short-lived. At day's end, the gallant veteran lost his prize to Chance, a younger red roan bachelor. Nevertheless, it was a very fine day for Raven—even though it was his last as a band stallion.

Cloud made no move to interfere with Santa Fe when he gently mounted Firestorm.

During the course of the summer, Santa Fe won other mares, but Cloud never again let him approach Firestorm. I have often wondered, *Would Cloud have been less possessive if Sitka had lived? Was she a mediating force in Cloud's life ... a balance to his controlling nature?* The proud and precocious colt I have followed and loved since the day he was born was revealing his deeply complex personality.

Cloud drove Santa Fe away, then brought Firestorm back to the family.

The Showdown

Just over the hill, I heard the shrieks of stallions in combat and rushed to see what was going on.

I found Bolder and Shaman rearing and screaming at one another. Shaman backed away and watched as Bolder defecated and smelled his droppings as if setting a battle line. Did the wordless message say, "Cross this line and I will attack you?"

Then, as if choreographed, the two stallions turned simultaneously. Like mirror images of one another, they walked in tandem with Bolder on the inside near the mares and Shaman on the outside. This intense interplay went on day and night, day after day, week after week.

In the meantime, the nose flies broke out by the billions, driving the horses crazy. The tiny flies seemed to cover every blade of grass. When the horses tried to graze, they inhaled the flies into their long noses and tried to dislodge them by violently shaking their heads up and down. Some bands started galloping madly as if trying to outrun their tiny tormentors.

Bolder's family sought relief in the cool of the forest where the flies were less numerous. Giant drifts, some even taller than the horses, lingered under the firs, creating a labyrinth of narrow passageways. Shaman followed the band into the maze, paralleling them when he could. I tried to keep up, trotting along

Opposite: Shaman dogged the band day and night, week after week.

Shaman peered out of the trees at the mares, his golden eyes aglow.

with my camera, crouching to grab a quick shot when I could. I was convinced that the maze was dangerous for Bolder and that Shaman would try to ambush the young stallion, separating him from the mares. A dark shape moving in the trees behind the band startled me. *Was it a bear?* Then I realized it was just Bigfoot scoping out the situation. Arthritic as he was, he seemed to believe he could still win a mare.

I caught a glimpse of tails flicking behind another grove of firs. *How many horses are in here?* I wondered. The tails belonged to Flint and his bachelor buddy, Cabaret. I watched them lurking behind the tall snowbanks. *One mistake,* I thought, *and you could be in trouble, Bolder.* The mares gobbled up some snow, then took a few bites of grass and moved on at a walk. When Bolder noticed Shaman in the shadows, he pressed the family into a trot. As they darted in and out of sunny openings and around the drifts, Flint moved in from the rear. When Bolder left to run him off, Shaman immediately rushed up to Cedar, and Bolder galloped back to drive him away.

Bigfoot stalked the forest edges, waiting for a mare to break ranks under the barrage of pressure and run from the group, but it never happened. Shaman dashed at Bolder through an opening in the trees, but Bolder charged right back at Shaman, and the older stallion backed away again. Finally, Bolder, the mares, and the foal made a run for the open meadows with Shaman trailing them at a trot.

Shaman and Bolder's cat and mouse game continued regardless of the inconsistent weather—rainy and cold one minute, sunny and warm the next. Quite suddenly one afternoon,

Bolder made a run at Shaman, reminding him to back off.

corn snow showered down. Bolder and the mares took to the trees as the hard little pellets of icy snow covered the magenta shooting stars and purple lupine that were nearly ready to bloom.

Almost as quickly, the sun came out and the band moved back into the meadow while Shaman used the cover of trees to move close to the band. I could see him peering out at the mares, his golden eyes aglow. *When would the gallant stallion make his move and take his family back? Had he already made a serious try?*

The band gradually moved to a ridgetop where a breeze blew the flies away. Cloud, too, traveled to the ridge with his family. The fillies were growing although Rain was much taller than Arrow, and I guessed she always would be. Bigfoot drifted in, staying on the perimeter of the bands. Bolder snaked his band into a tighter circle. Then he made a run at Shaman, reminding him to keep his distance.

Never wanting to pass up a good scuffle, Cloud arched his neck and walked proudly to his son. They sniffed and made a half-hearted, respectful little rear at each other. That's when Shaman moved forward and Bolder spun around, backing the bigger stallion downhill. But this time, Shaman struck back and the battle was on.

The two crashed into each other like linemen in a football game trying to get a leverage advantage. With teeth barred, they ripped at each other's coats, reared up and spun around, striking with their front hooves. Then they fell to their knees, trying to damage each other's legs. All the time they screamed and squealed angrily.

There is no comparison between a scuffle or a sparring duel and a full-blown fight. I wanted to escape the sound and the fury but kept filming. Shaman spun around and tried to kick Bolder in the face with his rear hooves, but Bolder was too fast, ducking under Shaman's legs. When Bolder stood up, he lifted Shaman off the ground! In trying to get off of Bolder's back, Shaman twisted, tripped, and ended up stumbling awkwardly downhill with Bolder giving chase. But the younger stallion veered away and rejoined the mares. Only Cascade paid any attention to the brutal fight; the other mares just continued to graze.

But this time Shaman struck back and the battle was on.

Although I was in awe of Bolder's speed and agility, I felt sorry for Shaman. He struggled back up the hill, walking stiffly. His neck was crooked to one side, an indicator of his pain. "Why didn't you kick Bolder out when he was a two-year-old?" I whispered over and over.

Bolder and his band moved away at sunset with Shaman walking far to the outside. I knew I had witnessed the passing of an era. Even Cloud had always showed great respect for the dun. Just last year, I watched Cloud resting in a small, deeply shaded opening in the forest to avoid the heat. When Shaman led his family into the same cluster of trees, Cloud retreated to avoid a confrontation with the senior stallion. Now, Bolder had succeeded in stealing his stepfather's family. I had never seen a stallion so young take over an entire band, let alone a band led by a legendary stallion.

Clearly, Bolder had inherited powerful genetics from his parents and grandparents. But beyond that, he had learned how to become a poised and powerful leader from the wise old stallion.

As the sun was setting, slanting rays of light shone in Shaman's golden eyes, and I was convinced I could see a tear.

Slanting rays of light shone in Shaman's eyes, and I was convinced I could see a tear.

Cloud courted his new dun filly.

Chapter 18

Shadow

The green meadows atop the mountain gradually dried into a sea of gold by autumn. The lupine went to seed while late blooming purple asters flowered in the once snow-filled ravines. I watched as diminutive pine squirrels scrambled high up into the fir trees and far out onto slender limbs, snipping off one sticky cone after another and tossing them to the ground. Climbing down, these small grayish-red rodents picked up one cone at a time and raced to bury them in their middens—mounds of shredded pinecones laced with tunnels at the base of big trees. They boldly guarded their middens, for the theft of the cones could mean starvation over the winter.

Clark's Nutcrackers were collecting nuts, too, but their favored cones were in the shorter limber pines. Like the squirrels, they cache their treasures in preparation for winter. I could see them flocking in trees out in the Forest Service lands near Tony's Island, a spectacular cliff-edged mesa with a lovely spring. At the base of the Island, I saw horses grazing and one of them sparkled in the morning light. It was Cloud. I hiked out to them and found that the family had grown.

Cloud walked behind his new dun filly. She was the stocky three-year-old daughter of Looking Glass. The filly had been with the bay stallion, Morning Star, and I wondered if Cloud had fought to win her? The Black walked with

Rain and Arrow were roaning out, light hairs mingling with dark.

her, helping Cloud to haze the filly back to the family. Suddenly, the filly broke away, and Cloud raced after her, his head dipped inches from the ground and his ears pinned flat against his head. He was able to turn her toward the band and she came to a halt. *He must have stolen her,* I thought. She did not seem one bit pleased at being in Cloud's family.

As the band started to walk in single file toward the water hole, Velvet took up the lead position, followed by Aztec. I took a long look at the usually trim grulla mare who looked chubby. All the horses had put on weight for winter and were growing thick coats. Both Rain and Arrow had really roaned out; their coats had turned far lighter than the month before.

I went ahead of the band, reaching the spring-fed water hole just as horses appeared on the rim above. Bolder and his family raced downhill with Shaman on the perimeter. The grand old stallion was still hanging out with the band, and Bolder didn't seem to mind. After they drank, I watched Shaman gently snake the dun foal back to the family as if he were a lieutenant stallion. *Surprising,* I thought. But I doubted that Shaman would be satisfied with playing second fiddle for long.

Then I saw a blue roan emerge over the hill. It was Velvet and the rest of the family following along in single file with Cloud pulling up the rear. Bolder watched his father coming in his direction and moved respectfully to the opposite side of the water hole. Cloud's band broke into a trot down the steep hill. Aztec moved with some difficulty,

Rain, above, and Arrow, right.

110

The buck's polished antlers gleamed in the morning light.

confirming what I feared. The mare was pregnant. After all these barren years, she was going to have a baby on the cusp of winter. I hoped she would foal soon – before the snows set in and the temperature plummeted.

Three weeks later, I returned to the mountaintop. Snow formed a necklace of white in the rocks rimming the teacup bowl. A herd of deer, both bucks and does, grazed some distance away. The biggest of the bucks raised his head and eyed me suspiciously. His impressive rack of antlers, polished free of their fuzzy velvet, shone in the angled morning light.

Movement in the trees caught my attention, and I hiked over to investigate. It was Cloud with his plump little fillies. Cloud had put on weight, too, and was growing a pristine winter coat that concealed his battle scars. On the outskirts of the band, the dun filly grazed peacefully, and I thought she seemed more comfortable with her new family. Then I saw Aztec walking from behind the trees. At her heels strode a dark foal. "You look like Rain," I whispered. She was dark sable brown like Rain had been as a baby, but she was stouter and her head was less tapered.

Over the next few days, I noticed that her personality was also different from Rain's. The baby was not as serious as her older sister who could be coaxed into play only occasionally by Arrow. Aztec's newborn needed no coaxing to kick up her heels. She was a spitfire, and her favorite game was the same as her

After all the barren years, she would foal on the cusp of winter.

111

"You look like Rain," I whispered.

father's when he was a baby. She loved to run! I watched her sprint at top speed through the trees, then gallop across the open meadows, zooming past Rain and Arrow, who looked so big in comparison to her. I named the spirited filly, Shadow, for her dark color.

Racing near Cloud one evening, she stopped abruptly, waited a beat, and walked right up to him. *Confident for a baby*, I thought. He sniffed her side and licked her coat sweetly. Then she bolted off. When I left the band well after sunset, I could make out a dark shape streaking through the trees and knew it was little Shadow.

The next day was cold with a biting wind out of the northwest. While searching for Cloud and the family, I encountered a mother black bear with a lovely white patch on her chest. She had two cinnamon cubs who were walking on the road above the bowl. When the cubs saw me, they ran to their mother who stood her ground and glared at me for a few seconds. She moved

The next day was cold with a biting wind out of the northwest.

112

Arrow could coax her serious sister into play.

her mouth open and shut in irritation. Once the cubs were safely behind her, all three rushed away. *What an absolutely beautiful trio!* Mother bear and her cubs would go into hibernation soon, escaping the worst of winter. But little Shadow and her mother could not escape the cold weather to come.

I found Cloud's family again in the limber pines and watched Shadow, wondering whether she could live through the coming cold and snow. Aztec would have to nurse her baby through these lean months, and I feared for her, too. *Maybe it will be a mild winter,* I hoped. I had no way of knowing that it would be the worst winter in a decade!

I wondered if Shadow could live through the coming cold and snow.

113

Seven years later, Trace and I were again searching for Cloud and his family.

Chapter 19

The Winter Search

In October, the snow began falling in earnest. By November, it blanketed the mid-ridges, but I could still drive halfway up the mountain. From Tillett Ridge, I hiked toward Big Coulee just as the blizzard began. Still, I tried to glass over onto Sykes. Above a rugged cliff face near the edge of Big Coulee, I spotted Cloud and dark horses foraging in the junipers. Then I saw a foal darting around in the trees. *Was it Shadow? It had to be her. Who else would be running in a blizzard?*

The snow continued into December and January. There was no way to drive into the horse range, so I tried another tactic. In February, I parked my horse trailer at the very bottom of the range in the desert. As I unloaded my wild horse, Trace, I watched his reaction. The handsome and steady blue roan, who had been born here and removed as a yearling, looked all around. I sensed he was happy to be home again. This was the fourth time I had traveled to the mountain with him. When he was just a green four-year-old, I rode him atop the mountain looking for Cloud. And here I was again, seven years later, searching once more for the pale stallion and his family.

I had no idea if Shadow was still alive. There had been no sightings of the band for months. With all the snow, I imagined that there could be horses in the low country, maybe even Cloud and the band, or Bolder, or Flint. I rode near the Bighorn Canyon and saw a pair of coyotes hunting on the snowy shores of the little lake that flows into the Bighorn River. They walked along, stopping frequently and cocking their heads, listening for the sound of mice and voles under the snow. One of the coyotes pushed his head into a drift. Coming up empty handed, he hurried to catch up with his mate.

Before the coyotes detected us, we moved on. Trace trotted right out whenever I asked him. He has always been a willing partner, full of confidence and curiosity. We climbed a gentle hill and sighted a small band of

The half-curl ram and one of the ewes walked over to nibble on the mountain mahogany bushes.

horses near the end of the lake. It was snowing lightly and magpies were sitting on the horses' backs. *What a good way to keep your feet warm,* I thought. The horses continued to graze, ignoring their feathered hitchhikers.

Farther north, we inadvertently rode up on a quartet of resting bighorn sheep. Amazingly, they didn't jump up and run away but kept chewing their cuds contentedly. Perhaps because there is little competition for food and they see wild horses all the time, they didn't view Trace as a threat. As for me, I felt invisible … just the way I like it. When the half-curl ram and one of the ewes got up and walked over to prickly mountain mahogany bushes, nibbling off their dark red leaves, we drifted quietly away.

The next day, Trace and I headed out to the bottom of Sykes Ridge near the spectacular red buttes. Just west of the buttes, we passed Sitting Bull, a dun stallion and his family, and kept heading west toward the mouth of Big Coulee canyon. When we climbed a flat hill where we could

Bolder and his family moved uphill through the melting snow.

scan the area called Turkey Flat, horses looked up at us … and I could not believe our good fortune. It was Bolder and his family! Shaman was conspicuously absent. I assumed he had finally given up any hope of reclaiming his family.

Unlike Sitting Bull's group, Bolder's band seemed nervous. As the sun broke through the clouds, they trotted away in the melting snow. I expected them to drop into the mouth of the canyon, but they started climbing the rocky ridge that paralleled Big Coulee.

When they were out of sight, Trace and I followed. This was new territory for me and, perhaps, for him, too. He had grown up on Tillett Ridge to the west, and I had never hiked this particular area before. Together, we began to explore, following the tracks of Bolder's band in intermittent patches of melting snow.

For days, we searched the area, finding a young stallion and his mare on the rocky side slopes of Indian Mesa. And near the drop-off into Cougar Canyon, we spotted a group of three bachelors, including the sabino stallion, Medicine Bow, who bore a scar across his forehead from a mountain lion attack. *But where was Cloud?* I fretted.

I knew Trace and I needed to get higher if we were to find Cloud. On the fifth day of our search, we started before sunup, traveling the same route Bolder had taken from the bottom. It was sunny and warm, and I was determined to get up on Sykes to find Cloud, Aztec, and the family. We climbed through broken junipers above

We spotted bachelors on a distant ridge..

117

Trace and I climbed higher on Sykes, determined to find out if little Shadow was alive.

determined to get up on Sykes to find Cloud, Aztec, and the family. We climbed through broken junipers above the mouth of Cougar Canyon, staying near the canyon wall. We stopped often, and I scanned west toward Tillett and east toward Syke's spiny ridgeline – a formation that had always reminded me of a giant lizard.

As we climbed above the canyon, we saw a grullo stallion and his band walking in single file through deep snow on the side of a treeless hill. Below them, in the deeper snow among the trees, were a dozen deer. They watched us but didn't run away. Trace struggled through near belly-deep snow, and I got off to hold onto his tail as he plowed forward, half dragging me up the mountain. The grullo stallion's band disappeared around the slope to our left, traveling uphill. On a beautiful day like today, I guessed that other horses would be moving up the mountain.

Trace and I kept climbing, detouring around a cave opening in the ground ahead. It was the entrance to Frogg's Fault Cave, a vertical drop of over 250 feet. I wondered how many animals had accidentally fallen into this death trap. Trace and I made a wide circle around the dangerous hole.

With difficultly, we slogged through deep snow in broken Douglas firs before we broke out onto a gently sloping meadow. We climbed to the top of the small, flat-topped hill. *Morning Star!* The bay band stallion and his family looked up as we quickly came to a stop. They stared at us as I pulled my binoculars out for maybe the hundredth time.

Trace is a wonderful platform for glassing because he stands perfectly still. I panned my glasses

118

Morning Star's band looked up and we quickly came to a stop.

over each family member. They looked fine and I noticed the particularly striking, blaze-faced grulla filly, Feldspar. Then the band drifted away, dropping over the edge of the meadow into upper Cougar Canyon.

After spotting Morning Star's family, I felt we had a good chance of finding Cloud's band. Over the years, the two bands would often graze on adjoining ridges, and I hoped this would be the case today. Trace walked on, and we did see more horses and some family bands but not the ones we were looking for. Time was running out. It was already afternoon and it would be dark in a few hours. I glassed one more time up on Sykes and saw a lone grullo horse. The horse was short-backed and in great shape. When he looked my way, I thought I saw a small star. I believed it was Flint. If only there had been more time, I might have been able to get close enough to confirm my guess.

Reluctantly, we turned around and made our way back to the mouth of Big Coulee, and although the light was failing, we made a fast dash into the canyon. Trace galloped through the sandy bottom where soaring walls put their rocky arms around us. I saw tracks but never the horses that made them. *Strange*, I thought. *Is Cloud somewhere other than Sykes ... but where?*

119

It was dark as we crossed Turkey Flat, but the sun still shone on the distant red buttes. A jackrabbit shot out of a sage at Trace's feet, and my steady blue roan friend just kept on walking. It was a great day, even if we didn't find exactly what we were looking for.

Later, I found out why our search for Cloud on Sykes was doomed to fail.

Chapter 20

The Hell 'n Gone

n March, based on a tip, I began to glass a rugged area far to the west of Sykes Ridge, adjacent to scenic Crooked Creek Canyon. It appeared to be a series of deep and impassable canyons. My friend, Trish Kerby, a longtime wild horse lover, dubbed the area the Hell 'n Gone. When glassing from Tillett Ridge west toward Crooked Creek Canyon, we often identified the dots as distant horses. But we could never figure out how we could get to them.

Now, years later, I sat on a rock west of Crooked Creek Canyon and peered to the east through my scope. This was a different vantage point of the Hell 'n Gone and gave me a more open view. I could see horse bands in meadows where the snow had melted or had blown away. I kept looking, tilting up to higher, snowier ridges. When I saw several suspicious looking dark spots, I zoomed in and focused. The dots were horses. *But what horses?* Then a light horse moved from behind a series of tall trees. It was Cloud ... no doubt about it!

I scanned the area around him again and again but only saw two other dark horses. *Maybe Velvet and The Black?* My heart sank. I feared that Cloud might have lost all but these two. I could not see any foals. I knew I had to try to find a way up there. I memorized landmarks, realizing that my perspective while hiking would be far different from my view down here. The old wooden fence between the BLM and Forest Service lands was a distinctive marker.

Cloud was above the fence at the edge of a dense forest with a canyon to the south. *I must remember … I must remember.*

The next day, I drove up Tillett Ridge Road, parked at the mines, and started hiking uphill in the snow. After an hour or so, I veered left when I saw the dilapidated fence line. Cloud would be to the northwest of here, if he hadn't moved. I tried to walk across areas where the ground was blown free of snow, or where the snow was just inches deep. Often I miscalculated and found myself in knee-deep drifts that I fought to get out of. I kept stopping, looking through my binoculars, and scanning the area above the fence. *A horse!* It stood on a side slope but then quickly walked out of sight behind trees. I knew it wasn't Cloud, but maybe it was a family member. I picked up the pace and, a few minutes later, I spotted Firestorm and beyond her, Cloud. They foraged on the edge of a cliff on the other side of a snow-clogged canyon.

I crossed on the high side of the canyon, above the trees with its waist-deep snow. It was a longer route but infinitely easier. Once on the ridge where I had seen Firestorm and Cloud, I kept walking uphill hoping to see Aztec and Shadow alive. Cloud appeared above me looking beautiful in his soft winter coat. I waved, and when he recognized me, he went back to eating the sparse, dry grass. I circled around him and saw The Black looking typically robust. Nearby, Dancer and Arrow foraged together ahead of me on a slight downslope in the snow. Rain and Velvet were nearby looking good, considering the severity of the winter.

Then I saw little Shadow atop the rocky ridge. The foal nuzzled her mother who lay flat on her side. My heart dropped, and I took a few steps forward and sat down. I

I spotted Firestorm and beyond her, Cloud.

Cloud recognized me, then went back to eating sparse, dry grass.

strained to see if Aztec was breathing. Shadow continued to nuzzle her. When the mare lifted her head, I let out the breath I had been holding since I saw her. Aztec stood up, and I could see how terribly thin she was with hip bones and shoulder blades that jutted out from her delicate frame. Shadow tried to nurse but gave up after a few seconds. Aztec had no milk. Her little daughter's coat was a mangy mess of light hair popping up through dark brown. Hours later when the wind picked up, Aztec lay down, and Shadow dropped down beside her mother's head. The two huddled together in the cold and wind. I left the family and started the hard walk back to the mines, whispering a little prayer, "Please let them live."

A month later, I returned when I could drive once again above the mines and through the old fence line I had used as a marker. I kept driving until I was able to glass downhill toward the Hell 'n

Shadow tried to nurse but gave up after a few seconds. Aztec had no milk.

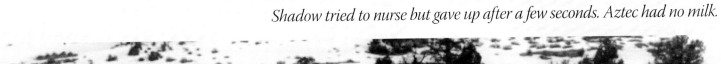

123

The two huddled together in the cold and wind.

Gone. From here, the ridges dropped at an angle toward Crooked Creek Canyon in deep, undulating waves. I could not identify the ridge where Shadow had lain with her mother, but I could see several posts jutting up and knew they were remnants of the old fence. There was no guarantee the family was still in that area, but they might be. And just as it started spitting snow, I began hiking down.

In less than a half hour, snow draped the junipers and covered the ground. In the trees below, I thought I detected some movement, but big wet flakes kept blowing into my face, making it hard to see. As I reached the edge of the open forest, Arrow wandered right by me like I wasn't even there. I wondered if snow was affecting her sight. Snow clung to her shaggy coat. When Cloud's dun mare walked through, I followed her. To my right, through a dreamy veil of snow, Cloud walked toward me out of the junipers looking like a mystical spirit horse. "Hello boy," I whispered and waved. He passed by, offering a token glance.

Cloud joined The Black who grazed nearby, and I caught a glimpse of Dancer and Firestorm in the blizzard. I walked around looking and hoping to find Aztec and Shadow. Instead, I discovered Velvet and started filming as Rain approached her mother to nurse, a sure sign that Velvet would not foal this spring. Something was coming behind the bushes to their left, and I panned the camera just as Shadow walked in. I wondered if she had any idea how good it was to see her. I could tell she was a bag of bones under her shaggy coat, but her eyes were bright. When I turned, I could see her mother, who had joined

Arrow wandered by me as if I wasn't there..

I wonder if Shadow knew how good it was to see her.

Cloud. Aztec was thin, but I believed that she and her baby had weathered the worst conditions that winter could have thrown at them.

As they all grazed together, the snow started to let up, and there was the hope of a clearing sky to the west. If Aztec and Shadow had been on their own, I doubt they would have survived. But together with their family, they found both the strength and will to carry on.

Chapter 21

Sykes Discoveries

In the second week of May, the weather flirted with sun and warmth ... but spring seemed to turn its back on the Arrowheads. Fog rolled through the canyons as I drove up Sykes Ridge on what I considered the worst road in the world! I have blown two tires and been stuck in the snow countless times while looking for Cloud. This time, I headed up the mountain in search of his son, Bolder.

I camped in a sheltered grove of trees. Even here, a swirling wind threatened to make a sail out of my tent. The rocks I cursed while driving became my friends at times like this. I piled them on anything I thought might blow away. Then I began to hike. By my calculations, Bolder could be a father around now. I had seen him breed his grulla mare, Cedar, nearly a year ago when I found them on their isolated island hideout.

In the afternoon light, I watched wispy clouds rising out of Big Coulee like plumes of smoke. Winter seemed unwilling to release its grip this spring. Still, I could hear the soft, swirling trills of mountain bluebirds on the wing and the insistent mating call of a male flicker in the dead snags below. I sat on a rocky hillside and glassed the upper ridges of Sykes, wondering if Bolder and his family were anywhere near me. In the trees on the next hillside, I spotted horses walking through the forest. They were both gray in color, perfectly

Flint had won a mare, and a beautiful one at that.

camouflaged amongst the trunks of Douglas firs. As they broke from the trees onto a trail below a rocky cliff, I saw the unmistakable blazed-face of the grulla filly, Feldspar, who had been with Morning Star. *But who is she with now?* When the other horse walked out from behind her, I gave a joyous silent cheer. It was Flint! He had won a mare and a beautiful one at that.

I heard that Feldspar had given birth, but there was no foal with her now. *Had a mountain lion killed it?* The two groomed each other affectionately as it began to drizzle. I hiked back to camp in the fading light, happy for Flint.

The next morning, I traveled on the wet trail below the rocky outcrop where I had last seen the new couple. Dense clouds cloaked the Bighorn Mountains and blocked the morning sun, keeping the temperature cold. I found Flint lying down and Feldspar grazing nearby. I sat down and watched the two. In time, Flint got up and stretched. He called softly to Feldspar in a low huffing voice. Then he walked over and quietly sniffed her ear. She made no move to escape his advances, and he mounted the mare. Afterward, they grazed together with their heads nearly touching.

I sat and watched these two young horses and imagined what their foal might look like next spring. The cheerful *dee-dee-dee* call of mountain chickadees in the trees around them erased

He talked softly to Feldspar in a low huffing voice.

the general gloomy weather from my mind, and I smiled at Flint, remembering him as a baby. The pale gray colt had been Cloud's little sidekick from the very beginning. When Flint looked up and stared over the hill, I was jarred back to the present. *What do you hear or smell, boy?* I got up and walked uphill in the direction he was staring.

As I crested the ridge, I saw a band of horses less than a hundred yards away. Bolder raised his golden head to look in my direction. "How incredible," I whispered in disbelief. *What were the chances of both sons grazing on the exact same ridge on the exact same day?* I hiked closer, hoping to get a better look at Bolder and his mares. The light dun yearling I named Honey came to stand with her stepfather, and they groomed gently. Texas grazed behind them while Cascade foraged nearby.

I circled around them, looking for the rest of the family. When I glanced downslope into the broken forest, I spotted a dun foal racing in circles around her mother. Texas's daughter, Autumn,

had given birth. The pretty little foal leaped over a stud pile and ran through the trees to her mother. She was the daughter of the hefty bay stallion, Mateo, who had bred Autumn the year before. I named the lively foal, Summer.

Then I saw Cedar walking uphill. At her heels was Bolder's daughter—a grulla filly foal with two perfect back booties. I named her Sage and noted her dorsal stripe, bold shoulder bars and leg stripes. These primitive markings are unusual in the domestic horse world but common on the Arrowheads. She had a rounded forehead called a ram's head, one of the typical head profiles of a Spanish horse.

Bolder raised his golden head to look in my direction.

129

I spotted a dun foal running around her mother.

Sage began to kick up her heals and raced through the trees. Cedar trotted behind her protectively but gave up when the filly just kept charging around, galloping past her young father and the others. Her gallop slowed to a walk, and she strode to Cedar to nurse. Then she lay down at Cedar's feet and slept. With Sage, Cloud became a grandpa for the second time.

I was so engrossed watching and filming the foals that I failed to notice the storm rolling across the mountaintop. Lightning lit up the clouds, and I took cover in the canyon behind me, hunkering down under trees on a steep slope. I hung onto low limbs to avoid sliding into the canyon while the lightning flashed and thunder crashed. Hail pounded down for a few minutes, and then rain came in sheets. Eventually, the weather cleared. It was a typically intense but brief mountain storm. When I crawled out of my slippery canyon refuge, the band had left. Thunder still rumbled, so I headed back to camp for the night.

The next day, I was unable to find Flint and Feldspar but located Bolder and his family grazing on the same ridge. While watching the two filly foals explore their surroundings, I heard Bolder scream, and I raced uphill to see him dueling with Flint. Apparently, Flint had approached the band in an attempt to steal a mare. Bolder deflected his attack and countered with one of his own, rushing after Feldspar. Flint dove at Bolder and then drove his young mare away with a nip at her rear. The confrontation was brief but

Sage began to kick up her heels and raced through the sage.

130

Bolder deflected Flint's attack and countered with one of his own.

worrisome. I feared that Flint ran the risk of losing Feldspar with this kind of impulsive challenge.

That afternoon, Bolder and his family moved nearer the road and farther away from Flint and Feldspar. I have no idea if Bolder was feeling any pressure, but I don't think so. The complexity of wild horse society continually surprises me. I sat with the band in the cold drizzle, observing how indifferent they were to the miserable conditions. When the rain started coming down in earnest, I retreated to camp. I knew that if the rain kept up, there would be no way to navigate safely down Sykes. I would be stranded.

In the morning, it was cloudy but the rain had stopped. I had intended to leave that afternoon, but when it looked sunny in the low country, I took advantage of this break in the weather and headed down the rugged road without a chance to say goodbye to Flint and Bolder. It made leaving the Arrowheads even sadder than usual. "Stay safe," I whispered.

I came over a rise and saw Cloud walking toward me.

Chapter 22

A Brief Affair

Broken clouds floated overhead creating a mosaic of sunshine and shadows on the open meadows of Tillett Ridge in late May. I came over a gentle rise and saw Cloud walking toward me with the sun shining on his beautiful pale yellow coat. Big Coulee was still in shadow behind him. He looked like someone had groomed his white mane and tail. *What a beauty*, I thought, as I had so often. From a higher point, I could see the rest of the family. Rain and Shadow were grooming each other, pulling tufts of dead hair from each other's motley coats. Shadow played with the clump of Rain's hair that was stuck in her mouth. She tried and tried to spit it out. And I laughed out loud when she finally gave up and swallowed it.

Arrow looked scruffy, too. When she walked to her mother, Dancer laid her ears back and bit at her daughter. *How odd*, I thought. Dancer was such a tolerant mother. Then I gave Dancer a good looking over. *You're pregnant*, I concluded, *and it's making you grumpy*. This time, the father would not be Prince but Red Raven. I had seen the two together when Arrow was little.

Both Firestorm and the dun mare looked pregnant, too. Firestorm would have a Santa Fe foal, and the dun mare's colt would belong to Morning Star. *No Cloud babies this year. Just grandkids for you old man*, I smiled. The beautiful stallion was clearly anything but old. He was in his prime as a

I was certain he had detected a mare in heat.

coming thirteen-year-old. Cloud nibbled at the first bits of green grass, late in sprouting after a bitter winter and a cold, wet spring.

He lifted his head and nickered softly, then started walking with purpose toward a grove of junipers and Douglas firs. I was certain Cloud had detected a mare in heat nearby, for I could hear him making a distinctive snuffling *huh, huh, huh* sound. The Black joined him. *What did she think she was doing?* They disappeared behind the junipers, then raced back into view. Both Cloud and The Black were chasing a chestnut mare and her two-year-old son. The mare kicked at Cloud, discharging a viscous spray. She and her son ran uphill with Cloud and The Black at their heels. The Black caught up to the mare, running beside her while Cloud drove the son away. The mare and The Black slowed down and stood together. They touched noses gently and I sensed The Black was calming her down.

Meanwhile, Cloud watched the hilltop, standing very still and listening intently. I think he expected the mare's band stallion to come sweeping over the rise to retrieve her. When he didn't come, Cloud walked to the chestnut mare and sniffed her flank gently, blew on her face, and spoke softly to her. I was close enough to hear his low, guttural vocalizations. This entire time The Black stood by the mare, steadying her. Then Cloud bred her.

Throughout the drama, Velvet and the rest of the family grazed amongst the broken trees and sage as if absolutely nothing was happening. Cloud urged the chestnut mare toward the family, and with The Black walking by her side, they moved closer to the band. I watched them for hours. Lakota, the mare's band stallion, never appeared, nor did their two-year-old son return to find his mother.

I had never seen anything remotely like this. I concluded that the chestnut mare had accompanied her son when Lakota kicked him out. Understanding The Black's behavior was more difficult. PZP had rendered her barren, robbing her of her natural role in the band. *Was she trying to contribute to the band in some other way? Did helping Cloud give her a purpose and a job to do?* She had functioned as a lieutenant stallion, but with a feminine touch—uncharacteristic and remarkable behavior in my experience.

The sun set over the Beartooth Mountains, and I packed up my camera gear and headed back down the rugged road. I could see the chestnut mare and Cloud and the rest of the family in the distance. Beyond them lay the deep red hills of Crooked Creek Canyon. Within days, the mare returned to Lakota. Her black son became a bachelor stallion. And Cloud's brief affair, made possible with the amazing help of The Black, was over. When I returned a few weeks later, an even bigger surprise awaited me.

The chestnut mare had been with Lakota and his mares for years.

Chapter 23

Cloud's Image

May 31st was a warm, sunny day. Flashes of bright sky blue darted by my window as I drove up the mountain. Male and female bluebirds flitted in and out of the sage and lit on the junipers, only to dart away again. Spring had finally arrived. I stopped to identify a lone bird perched in a dead snag. It was a male flicker, a species of woodpecker. I could see the dramatic red slashes on his cheeks. As he flew, I caught sight of the swept-back wings of a falcon diving toward him. "Peregrine," I whispered. The world's fastest diving bird was about to have breakfast. But, just before the falcon struck, the flicker twisted and rolled like a fighter pilot in a dogfight, shifting direction and flying to safety over the hill. *Lucky flicker,* I thought. I also felt lucky to witness this aerial matchup of predator and prey.

Farther up the mountain, where the tall trees begin, I saw mule deer wandering through the forest openings, browsing on an abundance of new growth. Clusters of pasque flowers blossomed at the edges of lingering snowdrifts, lifting their furry lavender heads to the sun. When the road got muddier and more snow packed, I parked and started hiking. The melodic mating trills of juncos atop the limber pines were punctuated by the harsh, drumbeat-like caws of Clark's nutcrackers. And in the distance, a pine squirrel chattered.

Mule deer wandered through the forest openings.

The tottering colt tried to keep up with his mother.

I reached the edge of the teacup bowl and looked down. In places, snow still covered the round, treeless meadow, and enormous drifts rimmed the cliff faces. A sharp *eek* rang out and I saw a marmot through my binoculars, sitting up on a rock looking back at me. *Busted*, I thought. His call was a *watch out* alarm signal to his kind – and every other wild creature within earshot.

Horses had been in the bowl. I could see their tracks in the snow. When I glassed to my right, I could just make out the roof of Penn's Cabin and a few dark horse dots on the distant meadows. The Bighorn Mountains, still buried in snow, rose just beyond. *It is bound to be a beautiful summer*, I thought, dreaming of the explosion of wildflowers to come.

I headed back down onto the mid-ridges of Tillett. Above the old Forest Service fence, I stopped to glass. There were horses near the road. I drove on and stopped again. It was Cloud! And I could see something else that looked white in the grass. What I saw next took my breath away. There was a white foal lying on the ground. I drove closer and stopped. Rain walked up to the colt and nibbled its back. It flinched. Rain, playfully but with a bit more force, nibbled the baby again. The foal struggled to get up. With difficulty, it stood on shaky legs and tried to walk. It was clear that I had missed its birth by only a few hours.

The disoriented newborn staggered after Rain, bumping blindly into her back legs. Then Dancer gently came to claim him. This Red Raven son had four white stockings, a long star, and

138

How could I not fall in love with a colt that looked so much like Cloud?

the faint block of pure white on his nose—an upside down version of Red Raven's unusual facial markings. But the colt was the color of Cloud as a baby ... not the spitting image of his grandfather, but nearly so. "Image ... Cloud's Image," I whispered.

The colt tried to keep up with his mother, bouncing against her as they walked. He was weak, so very weak that I worried he might not live. When he stopped, he hunched his back and pushed, straining to expel the little tar-like plug called the meconium, which must be eliminated before his first normal bowel movement.

While Image staggered around trying to pass the plug, Cloud walked over to an area of smashed down grass and began to sniff. This round spot was the place where the foal had been born. Dancer had already cleaned up the birth sac and the afterbirth, but the smashed grass remained—evidence that Image, like Dusty, had likely been born surrounded by his extended family.

Image stood all humped up, and pushed, finally passing the meconium. His relief was obvious as he tottered excitedly to his mother and nursed. Dancer was a good mother, but this foal would need extraordinary care, for he was not as strong as Cloud or Dusty had been. He would have the support of his strong, extended family and, perhaps, other foals to play with in a few weeks ... since the dun filly and Firestorm looked very pregnant.

Cloud continued inspecting the entire area of flattened grass, sniffing intently, and I wondered what might be going through his mind. He looked up as Dancer led the baby away. Image tried to keep up on his shaky legs. *So weak*, I thought. *I must not get too attached.* But how could I not fall in love with a colt that looked so much like Cloud?

Bolder and his family were heading toward a huge snow bank as Red Raven's little band moved away.

Chapter 24

Children of the Wild

Two weeks after Image was born, I drove up the mountain looking for Cloud, and hoping beyond hope that the colt had survived.

With growing excitement, I hiked to the edge of the teacup bowl and peaked over. You never know quite what to expect, and I was treated with a view of Bolder and his family on the far hill. They were heading toward a huge snowbank with Cascade in the lead. The two little fillies, Sage and Summer, wisely followed their parents around the drift. Cascade, on the other hand, decided to take a shortcut. She plunged into the deepest part of the drift. Finding herself mired in belly-deep snow, she flailed with all her might, sending a spray of snow in every direction before she succeeded in freeing herself. Bolder watched her, and I wonder if he thought the incident was as funny as I did. Cascade joined her band in gulping down huge mouthfuls of slushy snow.

Other horse families grazed below them in meadows of vibrant green. I spotted Prince with Electra, her new dark foal, Pococeno, and Winnemucca, one of the oldest mares on the Arrowheads. At over 20 years of age, Winnemucca was still round without any protruding ribs or hip bones showing. Her grulla coat shone steel-gray in the morning light.

Then I heard the shriek of stallions far to my right in the very bottom of

the bowl. It was Flint, and he was battling with the dark bay bachelor, Doc. They reared, pawed the air, and crashed down on each other as Doc challenged Flint for Feldspar. The pretty grulla filly stood just a few feet away from the stallions. Suddenly, Flint whirled and bit Feldspar's rear to get her going. The two of them galloped away down a slope still muddy from melting snow. Doc shook his long mane and forelock in agitation, but he did not chase after them. "Be careful, Flint," I cautioned under my breath.

As if in response to the excitement, Bolder's family took off at a gallop downhill. Cascade led the way, bucking in joy. The time of plenty had returned to the top of the Arrowheads, and the horses were on a protein high. Above the running horses, I noticed a lone horse watching. I looked through my binoculars. It was Shaman. The old stallion watched the family that once belonged to him and went back to grazing.

When I glassed the cliff edges below him, I spotted yellow-bellied marmots foraging on flowers and grasses that had popped out just in the past few weeks. On the cliffs where I sat, a marmot appeared above a small cave opening and sat upright. He was far lighter than the others, and when he turned to look up at me, I could see his pale face with white between his eyes, and his long, yellowed teeth. He was the old marmot I had photographed the year before. "Hello, gramps," I whispered, and took another picture of his aged face. He turned away from me, and stared down into the bowl.

I followed his gaze and watched Bolder. Dark patches now covered much of his body, and gray hair dominated his once flaxen tail. I missed his striking yellow coat, but I admired his calm, confident, peaceful demeanor.

Out of the corner of my eye, I caught something else moving and turned. Dark shapes tumbled out of a hole surrounded by sage. *Coyote pups!* The fuzzy babies rolled and pulled at each other, nipping and running in circles. Some dashed back down their hole to avoid the attacks of alpha litter mates. The most confident ones trotted away from the den to explore in the sage while others waited, looking far down the meadow. They were waiting for their parents, and so I waited, too, careful to move to a shaded spot with dark trees at my back.

Less than an hour later, I spotted movement in the sage. An adult coyote was heading for the pups. The adult traveled stealthily uphill, using a gully to disguise her approach. *Could it be one of the parents I'd seen the year before?* Judging by her size, it was the female. The pups saw her coming and rushed out, excitedly mobbing her as she neared the den. They jumped on her sides and licked at her muzzle, a behavior designed to elicit regurgitation. She looked up in my direction and I froze. Her right eye was missing. Now, I knew for sure it was last year's female. Unaware I was watching her, the mother coyote turned back to her pups and regurgitated her catch of barely digested voles.

The most dominant pup grabbed the biggest piece while the others competed for the remaining morsels. After breakfast, the mother coyote lay with her pups who nursed and then slept in the warmth of her body. After a while, she got up, stretched, and dashed off, disappearing into the sage and the forest below.

I had hoped that Cloud and his family would come to the bowl, too. But by noon, they were no- shows, so I set out to search for them. I spotted horses descending into a lovely, forest meadow surrounded by snow, and I followed them, unsure what band I was seeing. Then I saw Cloud in the rear with Dancer ahead of him. The white colt trotted at her side. *Image was alive!* Although he was a distance away, I could see he trotted with confidence; not at all like the weak foal of two weeks ago. He reared up at his mother and ran playfully in a circle around her as mule deer grazed peacefully behind them.

I noticed the dun mare was off to one side. *Still the outsider, aren't you girl?* She had foaled, for she looked much more slender. The baby must be lying in the grass somewhere nearby. I walked in a wide circle around the mare and sat down. When she walked off alone to join the band, I concluded that there was no foal, and I wondered if it had been killed by a mountain lion.

Firestorm's little filly had a huge gash on her shoulder.

Then I saw Firestorm trailing into the narrow valley with her new baby, a very pale bay. The little filly looked strong, and I thought she might resemble her father, Santa Fe, one day. *What a cutie,* I thought. When she turned, I gasped. The filly had a huge gash that extended from her right shoulder nearly to the top of her right leg. The wound oozed a greenish-yellow pus and looked infected. I was afraid it was a life-threatening injury. Yet, when the filly walked, she didn't limp. I watched her nurse her mother and explore the forest as if nothing were wrong. I wondered how she had escaped this obvious mountain lion attack. Against my better judgment, I named this Firestorm daughter and Cloud granddaughter, Ember.

Seconds later, the whole band exploded into a run. They excitedly rushed up a steep, rocky slope with The Black leading the way. Cloud pulled up the rear but stopped and turned around, staring into a forest of dark firs and deep snow. I looked into the trees, too. I explored this area many times and knew it well. It held the remains of foals. In years past, I discovered where mountain lions had cached their kills, covering the carcasses with sticks and leaves under trees at the base of a cliff. I named the forbidding forest, Cat's Cradle.

Cloud knew something lurked in the darkness. *Was it a cougar? And was it watching us?* After a minute, he turned and trotted uphill to join his family and I followed, looking back from time to time into the shadowy forest.

Seconds later, the whole band rushed up a steep, rocky slope.

Over the course of several days, I followed protectively along with Cloud's family. I was quite sure that Ember had somehow survived a cougar attack. *Was it the same cat that might have claimed the life of the dun's newborn? A juvenile cougar, perhaps?* An adult would surely have killed Ember, especially if it had wounded her in this way. I saw her biting at the wound. It had started to scab and looked oozy and infected. I watched how sweetly Image interacted with her. They groomed each other and walked side by side, obviously enjoying each other's company. I hoped Ember would make it.

One evening as a storm rolled through, Bolder's band grazed near Cloud's and all the foals began to play ... racing, spinning and bucking. Image burst into a gangly gallop and Shadow shot past him as if he were standing still. The filly had both spirit and speed. She trotted up to Rain to groom while Ember joined Image, dashing around him in the cold wind. One would never have guessed Ember had a huge wound on her shoulder as she ran circles around the pale colt. In response, Image jumped straight into the air and leapt back and forth as if playing tag with himself. Both foals raced to their mothers, nursed, then collapsed together in the grass.

Deep orange and black clouds raced over the horizon and the distant thunder rumbled. Bolder and his family began running uphill toward Bigfoot's sheltered valley. Their two foals galloped on the rim, lively silhouettes dancing and bucking. Although identifying color was nearly impossible, I knew I was looking at Sage when she kicked up her heels. Her two white booties caught the last of the red evening light, and then the band disappeared over the ridgeline.

Ember ran in circles around Image who jumped into the air.

145

Chapter 25

The Stallion King

A month later, I hiked to the edge of the teacup bowl hoping to catch a glimpse of the coyote pups. But there were none to be seen ... which came as no real surprise. The parents definitely would have relocated their young if they believed someone had discovered the den. This highly sensitive, adaptable, and intelligent species is also one of the most persecuted by humans. Despite systematic efforts to get rid of them, they have persisted, managing to outwit almost everyone. I can't help but admire them tremendously.

I drove on up the road. Standing on the lip of a hill, less than 100 feet away, was a pale grey adult coyote. He eyed me warily. *What a beautiful animal,* I thought, as I quickly got out my camera. I was confident it was the father of the pups. Through my long camera lens, I admired his gorgeous coat and his sparkling yellowish eyes. Orange, white, and yellow butterflies fluttered around his head. Then he turned away and dropped over the edge of the hill. The brief, magical moment was over. Struck by the wonder of this encounter, I was curious where he and his mate had stashed their pups. A moment later, I saw him again, loping away across a broad side slope where a single horse stood casually watching.

Using my big lens as a scope, I focused in on the dun stallion. It was Shaman.

Cloud's band began heading for water.

He stared downhill, not at the coyote but at something else that I couldn't see. I needed a better angle and hiked to a spot where I could see the slope just below me. It was Cloud and his family. A quick head count revealed that they were all present and accounted for. Rain and Shadow were grooming each other, as they so often did. Ember was behind Image, waiting for him to finish nursing. Both foals had grown, and I trained my long lens on Ember, hoping to see if that nasty gash was healing. When she turned her right side toward me, I looked at the wound in amazement. Not only had it healed, it was hardly noticeable. In its place was an area of lighter hair and a thin, almost imperceptible line where the tear had been. *What incredibly resilient animals,* I thought. The rest of the family was grazing peacefully when Cloud looked up at horses on the rim.

Bolder and his mares marched out in single file with the two little fillies trotting to keep up. Their determined walk convinced me they were heading for water. Beautiful Cascade led them over the hill and out of sight.

When Image finished nursing, Cloud's band began walking uphill in the direction Bolder's family had taken. I guessed they, too, were heading for water. Shaman had dropped off the hill and began following Cloud's band. Cloud stopped, letting his family continue alone. He stared back at Shaman who stopped when he saw Cloud looking at him. For at least a minute, Cloud watched the dun before turning to catch up with the band. When Cloud wasn't looking, Shaman followed,

Cloud stared back at Shaman before turning to catch up with the band.

staying a distance back. At the top of the hill, Cloud stopped once again and looked back. Shaman abruptly stopped and started grazing. When Cloud dropped over the hill, Shaman walked up the same narrow trail Cloud had taken. *Was Shaman actually dogging Cloud?*

I hurried, trying to get to the water hole before Cloud did. I could see Bolder drop into the basin that held the snow-fed pond, but Cloud's band kept coming. With Cloud in the rear, they approached the shallow red water hole near Penn's Cabin where Mescalero and his little family were drinking. When Cloud trotted to the front of his band, Mescalero and his family alertly and respectfully trotted away.

Cloud waded into the middle of the shallow, red depressions, splashed a few times, then flopped down and rolled, turning his pale coat into a muddy, red mess. The mares waded in and began to play when Cloud unexpectedly dashed out of the pond, sending rivulets of red water in all directions. He rushed past Image and stood on a little rise. He could see Shaman crossing the wide meadow.

Cloud walked to a red dirt wallow near the water and rolled, caking his wet coat with red dirt, and staining his mane and tail a bright orange. He kept a wary eye on Shaman the entire time. The mares moved off a bit to graze while the foals lay down, rolling onto their sides for a snooze in the warm sun. But Cloud was suspicious of Shaman and kept watching him. The old stallion made a wide circle around the band and went to the exact spot where Cloud had rolled. He smelled the area thoroughly and then rolled, covering Cloud's scent with his own. When Shaman walked to the water's edge to get a drink, Cloud exploded into a gallop, attacking him ferociously with teeth barred and ears pinned flat against his head. The older stallion raced through the water to get away, but Cloud was on him in a flash. Shaman reared and struck out defensively. When Cloud dove at him again, Shaman pivoted and ran away.

Instead of chasing him, Cloud trotted back to his band and snaked all of them away from Shaman … all but Image, that is. The foal slept soundly in the grass. Clearly sacked out, the colt wasn't moving a muscle, and Cloud approached him with his head held low to the ground … a clear signal to get

Image promptly corrected course with Cloud still in determined pursuit.

going. When Image finally woke up, he leapt in the air and ran—in the wrong direction! He galloped toward Shaman. Cloud raced behind him, nipped the terrified colt on his rear end, and circled around him. Image promptly corrected course with Cloud still in determined pursuit of the colt. That's when Dancer rushed in and took charge of her son, ushering him at a trot toward the safety of the mares.

At first, I thought Cloud's behavior was brutal, but when I had more time to reflect on this severe reprimand, I realized what an important lesson this was for Image. Paying attention and moving quickly to stay with the family might make the difference between life and death. I think Image will always remember this. Maybe, someday, he will pass this lesson on to his own son or daughter.

As for Shaman's actions that day, I'm still left wondering. *Why would such a smart and savvy veteran pick a formidable stallion like Cloud to dog? Did he really believe he could steal a mare away from him?* Regardless of his reason, I never saw him challenge Cloud again. I felt I had witnessed Shaman's last hurrah … one last effort to reclaim what he had cherished his entire life—a family.

Over the next few days, I sat above the snow-fed water hole as band after band appeared on the wide meadows and raced to the water. Dozens of horses at a time splashed and rolled in the pond. What fun for them on a warm day! The pale dun stallion Chino and his beautiful family raced downslope toward the water hole, followed by the grullo stallion Lakota and his colorful band. As new

Flint looked down at the horses around the pond and I followed his gaze.

My heart dropped. Flint had lost his mare to Prince.

horses arrived, others left, taking turns at having a drink and cooling off.

I noticed Custer above the water hole with Flint. *What was Flint doing up there? He should be with Feldspar.* As Flint looked down at the horses around the pond, I followed his gaze. Prince was leaving the water with Electra and her foal, along with the older mares, Winnemucca and Pococeno, and one other. I could see the grulla filly's big blaze. It was Feldspar. My heart dropped. Flint had lost his mare to Prince.

I looked back up at Flint who watched as Feldspar followed Electra a short distance from the pond. Feldspar started to groom with Electra's foal. *Oh my,* I thought, *the young filly likes being with this family.* She has other females as friends and even a baby to make up for the loss of her own. *This will be hard, Flint.* Still, when I had watched the filly with Flint in May, I sensed an emotional attachment between the two. I hoped he would somehow win her back.

The sound of thundering hooves roused me out of my romantic reflections. Horses were coming. I looked to the steep slope beyond the water hole to see Cloud's band racing downhill! I could see Velvet and Rain, Aztec and Shadow, Dancer, Arrow and Image, Firestorm and Ember, and the dun filly. Then Cloud suddenly appeared. He galloped downhill or was he floating? His gait was effortless even though he was descending a precipitous hillside. The mud had fallen from his coat and he appeared nearly white, as if someone had spent considerable time grooming him for just such a dramatic entrance.

His family curved onto the hill above the water hole and started to graze in brilliant green grass. A huge snowdrift covered the slope only days before, and it seemed like the fresh grass had popped up overnight.

Cloud did not join them. He stopped and looked over at Flint. *Here we go again*, I thought. After all this time, Cloud still went into high alert at the sight of his stepson. He pranced to Custer and Flint, and the three sniffed noses and screamed. The two bachelors trotted away with Cloud following them, daring them to fight. When he couldn't get a rise out of Flint or Custer, he trotted back to Velvet. In time, the family went to water together. And when they did, all the other bands moved away. They drank from the pond, rolled and circled the water hole, headed up in my direction, and stopped to graze just below me. I watched Image and Ember groom each other sweetly at sunset. Then the two foals lay down in the flowers, enjoying the last warm rays of sunlight.

On the other side of the pond, Bolder's band moved down for a drink and then climbed back up hill into the emerald grass. The two little fillies, Summer and Sage, looked plump. Sage had grown even taller and leggier than when I last saw her. She reminded me of her great grandfather, Raven, who had disappeared during the past winter. I knew he was dead, and I will always miss him … but I will forever cherish the astonishing legacy he left behind.

At sunset, when the other horses had left the water hole, Shaman came down alone and drank. I watched him walk away, the angled sunlight shining red through the dust kicked up by his hooves. I know that one day I will see Cloud walking away alone. But that won't be for a very long time, I hope. For now, it is his time to reign, and no matter his destiny, I pray I will be here to share in the freedom and wildness of his mountain home.

The sun sank over the horizon, and billowing white thunderheads turned orange, then deep red and, finally, deep purple. Before night swallowed them up, I saw Cloud with his family walking atop a high hill, silhouetted against the wide Montana sky. *Good night, boy,* I whispered.

The Cloud Foundation

In order to prevent the extinction of mustangs on our public lands and particularly Cloud's herd, Ginger Kathrens formed The Cloud Foundation, Inc. in 2005. The 501(c)3 non-profit foundation relies exclusively on donations from the public which are tax deductible.

We invite you to join us in our battle to preserve these magnificent animals. Visit www.thecloudfoundation.org to learn more about what you can do to keep Cloud and all wild horses roaming free on OUR public lands.

Proceeds from this book, _Cloud: Challenge of the Stallions_, will be used to fight on behalf of wild horses and their right to live free. Kathrens' first two books, _Cloud :Wild Stallion of the Rockies_ and _Cloud's Legacy: The Wild Stallion Returns_ as well as the DVD's of all three Cloud films are available for a donation to the Foundation.

www.thecloudfoundation.org

Cast of Characters

Adona: Blue Roan daughter of Shaman and Sitka. With Red Raven and Blue Sioux. Barren mare-given infertility drugs as a yearling and two-year-old

Arrow: Bay roan daughter of Cloud Dancer and Prince. Cloud granddaughter

Aztec: Grulla daughter of Black Beauty and Beauty. Cloud's mare and mother of Shadow

Autumn: Daughter of Texas and Shaman. Born out-of-season. Mother of Summer.

Blue Sioux: Blue roan Red Raven mare. Former Plenty Coups mare

Beauty: Grulla mother of Aztec. Black Beauty's mare

Bigfoot: Dark bay former band stallion. Old and arthritic but spirited

Black Beauty: Black band stallion and father of Aztec

Bo: Black bachelor stallion who dogs Bolder. Son of Boomer and Coppertop

Bolder: Palomino son of Cloud and Pococeno. Shaman step-son

Boomer: Black band stallion. Father of Bo

Cabaret: Grullo bachelor stallion. Son of Looking Glass

Cascade: Black-brown mare with cascading mark down face. Shaman then Bolder mare

Cedar: Grulla mare with Shaman and then Bolder. Mother of Sage

Chance: Red roan bachelor stallion and band stallion. Captures Santa Fe's band

Chino: Buckskin band stallion

Cloud: Pale palomino son of The Palomino mare and Raven. Band stallion. Flint's stepfather

Coppertop: Sorrel mare with Boomer. Mother of Bo

Custer: Bay roan band stallion and bachelor. Son of Shaman and Sitka

Dancer: Blue roan daughter of Cloud and Sitka. Mother of Arrow and Image

Diamond: Blue Roan half brother of Cloud. Band stallion injured during bait trapping

Doc: Dark bay bachelor stallion. Son of Winnemucca and Mateo. Challenges Flint for Feldspar

Dusty: Buckskin son of Cloud and Velvet. Killed by mountain lion during bait trapping

Electra: Red Roan half sister of Cloud with lightning bolt mark on face. Mateo then Prince mare

Ember: Light bay daughter of Firestorm and Santa Fe. Cloud granddaughter

Feldspar: Blaze-faced grulla daughter of Starman and Rosarita. Flint's mare.

Firestorm: Light red roan daughter of Velvet and Cloud. Mother of Ember

Flint: Grullo roan son of Shaman and Sitka. Cloud step-son

Gemini: Orange filly foal daughter of Diamond and The Palomino mare. Killed by mountain lion during bait trapping

Halo: Bay filly daughter of Corona and Waif. First born foal of 2007

Helena Montana: Grulla filly daughter of Seattle and Bakken. Second born foal of 2007

Honey: Light dun filly daughter of Shaman and Cedar. Raised by Bolder

Image: Pale palomino son of Dancer and Red Raven. Grandson of Cloud

Lakota: Grullo band stallion. Chestnut mare that Cloud courts is in his band

Looking Glass: Older dun band stallion. Father of Cabaret

Mateo: Dark bay band stallion and bachelor. Father of Summer

Medicine Bow: Sabino bachelor stallion. Survived mountain lion attack

Mescalero: Dun roan band stallion. Son of Shaman and Sitka

Morning Star: Dark bay band stallion. Feldspar was in his band in 2007

Plenty Coups: Blue Sioux and Pococeno were his mares. Injured during fights with Cloud in 2001. Lost his family. Killed by lightning. Named for last great Crow chief

Prince: Dun band stallion. Lost family in 2003. Regained mares, including Electra. Father of Arrow

Pococeno: Black mare in Plenty Coups' band. Stolen and bred by Cloud in 2000. Stolen from Cloud by Shaman in 2000. Mother of Bolder. With Prince's band 2007

Rain: Brown roan filly daughter of Velvet and Cloud

Raven: Black band stallion. Injured in 2005 and lost his mares. Father of Cloud, Red Raven, Diamond, Electra and Cedar. One of the most dominant and prolific of the Arrowhead stallions

Red Raven: Red roan band stallion. Son of Raven. Half brother of Cloud

Sage: Grulla daughter of Cedar and Bolder

Sandman: Older Dun band stallion and bachelor

Santa Fe: Bay band stallion. Father of Ember

Shadow: Brown roan daughter of Aztec and Cloud. Born out-of-season

Shaman: Older dun band stallion and bachelor. Dominant and prolific band stallion. Bolder's stepfather

Sitka: Older blue roan mare. Long time Shaman lead mare then Cloud lead mare.

Sitting Bull: Dun band stallion in desert

Starman: Blaze-faced bay band stallion. Father of Feldspar

Summer: Dun filly daughter of Autumn and Mateo. Granddaughter of Texas and Shaman

The Black: Black daughter of Velvet. Barren after infertility injections as yearling and two-year-old. Stolen from Prince by Cloud

The Palomino: Palomino mother of Cloud

Texas: Dun mare in Shaman's band. Texas-shaped star. Bolder mare. Mother of Autumn

Trace: Blue roan son of War Bonnet and Opposite. Captured in 1997 as a yearling and adopted by author

Velvet: Blue roan mare captured by Cloud in 2003. Mother of Firestorm, Dusty, and Rain

Winnemucca: Older grulla mare with Mateo and then Prince. Mother of Doc

Glossary

blaze: white stripe on face that runs from between the eyes to the nose

blue roan: black and white body hair mixed together; black head, mane, tail, and legs

bay: shades of reddish brown with black points, black mane and tail

bay roan: reddish brown and white body hair mixed together: brown head, mane, tail, and legs

buckskin: yellow or tan body with black points

claybank buckskin: pale buckskin; color matches the riverbanks near the Arrowheads; sacred color to some Native American tribes

dogging: stalking

dun: used here for zebra dun with primitive marks over withers; body color tan to dark golden brown with black mane, tail, and legs

forelock: long hair that falls over the face or between the ears

grulla: silver gray to slate gray body color with primitive marks of dorsal stripe, leg stripes, and stripe over withers; Spanish word for sandhill crane colored

grullo: male of this color

mahogany bay: dark red bay

palomino: various shades of yellow with light mane and tail

points: edges of the ears, mane, tail, and lower legs; all horses have either black points (duns, grullas, bays) or non-black points (sorrels, red roans, palominos)

primitive marks: dorsal stripe, leg stripes, and shoulder bars

red roan: red and white body hairs; red head, mane, and tail

roan: white and a color mixed on the body; head, mane, and tail are the nonwhite color

sabino: flecking of small spots of white on the back ground color

snip: a white or pink mark between a horse's nostrils, extending into or near the nostrils

sorrel: red body; red to near white (flaxen) mane and tail

star: white mark on forehead